PATIENT-PERSPECTIVE CARE

A NEW PARADIGM FOR
HEALTH SYSTEMS AND SERVICES

TIMOTHY A. CAREY

I0130943

R Routledge
Taylor & Francis Group

LONDON AND NEW YORK

First published 2018
by Routledge
2 Park Square, Milton Park, Abingdon, Oxon OX14 4RN

and by Routledge
711 Third Avenue, New York, NY 10017

Routledge is an imprint of the Taylor & Francis Group, an informa business

British Library Cataloguing-in-Publication Data
A catalogue record for this book is available from the British Library

Library of Congress Cataloging-in-Publication Data
Names: Carey, Timothy A., author.
Title: Patient-perspective care : a new paradigm for health systems and
  services / Timothy A. Carey.
Description: Milton Park, Abingdon, Oxon ; New York, NY : Routledge,
  2018.
Identifiers: LCCN 2017040428| ISBN 9780815378778 (hbk) |
  ISBN 9780815378785 (pbk) | ISBN 9781351227988 (ebk)
Subjects: LCSH: Patient participation. | Health services administration. |
  Health planning.
Classification: LCC R727.42 .C35 2018 | DDC 610.69/6—dc23
LC record available at https://lccn.loc.gov/2017040428

ISBN: 978-0-8153-7877-8 (hbk)
ISBN: 978-0-8153-7878-5 (pbk)
ISBN: 978-1-351-22798-8 (ebk)

Typeset in Bembo
by Apex CoVantage, LLC

PATIENT-PERSPECTIVE CARE

Inappropriate health care is an escalating and expensive problem. It affects high-, middle-, and low-income countries, wastes billions of dollars annually, and harms individuals and communities. Inappropriate care refers to both the *overuse* and *underuse* of tests and treatments and, ironically, can occur concurrently within the same health system. Even though patient-centred care is still the prevailing ethos, specifying where patients should be situated geographically has not required health professionals to consider the preferences, values, and priorities of patients when making treatment decisions.

Patient-perspective care demands that the decisions health professionals make are in the service of patients' goals. Health care, ultimately, is helping individuals to live the lives they would wish for themselves. To meet this imperative, health professionals must work towards understanding what their patients would like to achieve through their engagement with health services. This book details the extent and scope of inappropriate care and how we have arrived at this position. The necessity for patient-perspective care is outlined and provides a theoretical framework that explains why patient-perspective care is so critical. The implications of this theory are then explored, and specific strategies for moving towards a patient-perspective approach are discussed.

This book is entirely original and describes a novel, fresh approach to delivering health services. Many long-standing and expensive problems such as missed appointments will disappear, and patients will be more satisfied with the treatments they receive. Health services generally will be more efficient and effective, leading to more sustainable and affordable health care.

Timothy A. Carey is the director of Flinders University's Centre for Remote Health. He is a clinician, teacher, and researcher who has developed the Method of Levels, an a-diagnostic, personalised psychotherapy which is described in the book *Principles-Based Counselling and Psychotherapy: A Method of Levels Approach* (Routledge 2015).

To Margaret and Jack
Best woif ever, best kid ever
Love yous mob

Contents

LIST OF TABLES   IX

PREFACE   X

1   Our global health crisis   1

2   How have we arrived at this position?   10

3   Why has the concept of patient-centred care failed?   17

4   The importance of the patient's perspective   32

5   The theoretical underpinnings
    of patient-perspective care   44

6   What patient-perspective care means in practice   55

7   Patient-led appointment scheduling: a practical
    example of patient-perspective care   82

8   Patients' perspectives   96

9   Where to from here?   122

INDEX   131

TABLES

6.1 Differences between the patient-centred and patient-
     perspective approaches to health care.   56
6.2 Patient-perspective health care characteristics and their
     implications for practice.   58
6.3 Statements of self-determination and rights to refuse
     treatment in ethical codes of different psychological
     societies and associations.   66
7.1 Early studies of psychological treatment reporting
     durations and frequencies of treatment.   89

PREFACE

Be careful. Caution is advised as you embark on the journey of this book. This book contains a new and dangerous idea. The idea is new because it is based on a very different account of how humans conduct the business of day-to-day social living. Actually, this new explanation has been available to us since the 1960s, but it is still not very well known. Even by people who purport to know about it, the elegant and robust principles are often misunderstood and distorted to make them more like the comfortably familiar stories of the status quo.

The idea in this book is dangerous because it is a radical departure from what has gone before. The radical departure, though, is not really the most dangerous part. The idea to be outlined in this book is especially dangerous because, in some ways, it might seem like it's just building on, or even complementing, past or current initiatives. It's not. While it's true that there are some current programs and practices that are entirely consistent with the approach that is mapped out in this book, for the most part, these efforts occur as isolated innovations. What is needed is an overhaul of the entire system. Small pockets of wisdom will not be enough to refashion health services across the globe.

In some ways, the structure of this book might seem counterintuitive. I have not started with a description of the new approach. Rather, I begin the book by comprehensively outlining why such sweeping change is needed. In the first few chapters, I discuss the global crisis of inappropriate health care. The harm being caused to people and the billions of dollars being wasted must stop. Against the background of inappropriate care, I offer some suggestions as to why the concept of patient-centred care has failed so thoroughly. I then outline why the patient-perspective approach is the solution that we need, and I provide a compelling theoretical justification for the sensibility of this new direction.

In Chapter 6 I discuss in a general sense some of the practical implications of implementing the patient-perspective approach, and in Chapter 7 I provide a specific example of clinicians adopting a patient-perspective system of scheduling appointments for psychological treatments. Chapter 8 provides the perspectives of five patients who have had less than ideal experiences with the health system along with their suggestions for how things could be improved. In all cases, the suggestions can be distilled down to the common factors of ensuring that the design and delivery of health care is driven by the priorities, values, and preferences of the patients.

If you're already convinced that a radical change is required, you can skip over the first few chapters. If you find yourself questioning just how pervasive we need the change to be, however, you might benefit by returning to the earlier chapters and reflecting on the seriousness of our current situation and how we might have situated ourselves in this dire position. The extent to which both over-treatment and under-treatment are occurring is truly breathtaking. It is, at the same time, unacceptable and unsustainable. Despite the seriousness of our current situation, there will still be resistance to an all-encompassing system redesign. It was my anticipation of resistance that led me to the decision to build the argument slowly, systematically, and deliberately.

It is because of how embracive the change needs to be that it is not until Chapter 6 that the differences between the patient-centred and the patient-perspective approaches are finally highlighted. First, the foundations needed to be laid. Without this elemental information, the words in the subsequent chapters would not make as much sense.

Before you set off on this literary adventure of conceptual and structural reform, a note about terminology is warranted. Throughout this book, the term "patient" is used. I chose to use this term because this book is about health care in general. I could also have used the term "client", although "patient" is perhaps in more general use throughout the health system. Actually, my favourite term is "person", but if "person" is to be used, it becomes cumbersome and overly wordy to constantly refer to "the person providing the service" and "the person receiving the service". Moreover, "patient" is appropriate in another subtle but crucially important way as well. While there is much to admire about what we have achieved in health care across the ages, we have also got it wrong in spectacular ways as evidenced by the staggering amount of money being wasted on inappropriate care. People can be harmed as a result of receiving inappropriate care so, people receiving services have had to be exceedingly *patient* while the people designing, developing, and delivering services have fumbled about trying to get it right.

This book is about getting it right. It presents a more efficient and effective way of getting it right, but the catch is that getting it right doesn't necessarily entail changing our strategies or services. Real change involves shifting our attitudes, our goals, and our perspectives. And these changes might be the hardest changes of all. Perhaps it is this aspect of the patient-perspective paradigm that is the most dangerous and challenging aspect of all. Will we, en masse as health professionals, have the tenacity and fortitude to do what is required to change our attitudes and opinions for the chance to get it right? You might be in a better position to answer this question when you get to the end of the book.

1

OUR GLOBAL HEALTH CRISIS

Globally, our health systems are in an enduring and escalating crisis. The inefficiencies in our systems, brought about by the provision of inappropriate care, are devouring enormous amounts of financial resources. In some ways, we are the victims of our own successes. While modern medical care has yielded many remarkable achievements and progressed the health of populations around the world, this improvement in health has brought with it an increase in health care spending (Saini, Brownlee, Elshaug, Glasziou, and Heath, 2017). A challenge that is genuinely international is the development and delivery of better value health care – how can health care systems provide improved health per dollar spent (Saini, Brownlee et al., 2017)?

The pervasiveness and cost of inappropriate care

Inappropriate care is a long-standing and pervasive phenomenon (Saini, Brownlee et al., 2017). A paradox that has been relatively neglected can now be identified which affects high-, middle-, and low-income countries. This seemingly contradictory conundrum is *the failure to deliver needed services in conjunction with the continued provision of unnecessary services* (Saini, Brownlee et al., 2017). In 1998, Chassin and Galvin described the underuse, overuse, or misuse of treatments as a serious and widespread problem in the United States of America (USA) with many people being harmed as a result. Based on conservative estimates, the overall financial waste in USA health care was estimated to be $558 billion in 2011 (Berwick and Hackbarth, 2012), and in 2013, at least $270 billion was spent just on health care that could be defined as overuse (Brownlee et al., 2017). The overuse of medical services is not limited to the USA. According to Brownlee et al. (2017, p. 8), "There is strong evidence for the widespread overuse of several specific medical services in many countries, suggesting that overuse is common around the world and might be increasing". In both high-income countries as well as middle- and low-income countries, simple and inexpensive interventions are underused, while interventions that are "ineffective but familiar, lucrative, or otherwise convenient services, despite potential patient harms" are overused (Saini, Brownlee et al., 2017, p. 1).

Defining important terms

Chassin and Galvin (1998) provided definitions for the terms "overuse", "underuse", and "misuse". Overuse arises in situations when the potential for harm of providing a health care service exceeds the benefit. Prescribing antibiotics for viral infections or prescribing antidepressants for mild depression could be considered examples of overuse. Underuse is the situation when a health care service fails to be provided when it would have produced a favourable outcome. An uncompleted childhood immunisation protocol is an instance of underuse. Misuse refers to situations when a preventable mishap occurs in an otherwise appropriate service, resulting in the patient not experiencing the full benefit of the service. Avoidable surgery complications or a patient developing a rash after receiving penicillin despite a known allergy to the drug are examples of misuse.

The grey zone

While it is useful to have clear definitions of terms, the direct application of Chassin's and Galvin's (1998) definitions is complicated by what has been described as an ambiguous grey zone in health care (Brownlee et al., 2017). For most health services, the probability of benefit or harm is uncertain for any individual (Saini, Brownlee, et al., 2017) and is influenced both by the characteristics and capacities of the individual, as well as environmental contexts within which the individual functions. Patients, therefore, differ in the extent to which they assess their various treatment options as well as the trade-offs that may be required for the chosen treatment (Blank, Graves, Sepucha, and Llyewellyn-Thomas, 2006).

Given these definitional difficulties, direct measurement of appropriate and inappropriate care is less than straightforward. Even within the context of these measurement considerations, however, in high-income countries, across a wide range of services, the high prevalence of overuse is well documented (Brownlee et al., 2017). Furthermore, overuse is detected at increasing rates in low-income countries. The harms of overuse to both the individual and the health system cannot be overstated. Patients can be harmed physically as well as psychologically, and health systems can be harmed through the waste of resources and the diversion of investments in both public health and social spending (Brownlee et al., 2017). While the severity of overuse should not be underestimated, underuse is also associated with serious problems when patients and populations are left in a vulnerable position with respect to avoidable disease and suffering (Saini, Brownlee et al., 2017).

No doubt numerous factors contribute to the existence of the grey zone. Whatever the factors are that led to its manifestation, however, it is the outcomes within the grey zone that are so problematic for the provision of appropriate care. There can be tremendous variability across patients in the amount of benefit extracted from many interventions. The balance between benefits and harms, for example, varies substantially for adolescents who are prescribed antidepressant medication (Brownlee et al., 2017). Compounding the problem is the fact that some interventions, such as glucosamine for osteoarthritis of the knee, can be popular despite offering little benefit to most patients (Brownlee et al., 2017). Finally, services that are backed by scant evidence – many screening tests may fit this category – offer little guidance as to which patients might benefit and by how much (Brownlee et al., 2017).

It is perhaps the ambiguity inherent in the grey zone that makes patient values and preferences so critical for determining appropriate care in many situations (Brownlee et al., 2017). In fact, it is hard to imagine how care could be judged to be appropriate or otherwise *without* regard to a patient's preferences, values, and attitudes. The fact that inappropriate care is so widespread strongly suggests that patient values and preferences are not as central to health care service provision as they should be. Engineering the ways in which patient preferences can be brought to centre stage in the context of health care service provision may well be the most pressing problem currently facing health systems. Saini, Brownlee et al. (2017) maintain that a crucial pathway to authentic health care affordability is being able to define the right care as well as understanding the forces that work against it. Failure to navigate this pathway "will leave universal access to high-quality, cost-effective, and compassionate care an ever-receding mirage" (Saini, Brownlee et al., 2017, p. 1).

What defines appropriate care?

The primacy of the patient's perspective is inescapable when concepts such as "appropriate care", "inappropriate care", and "right care" are discussed. Yet even within these discussions, it is possible to gain some sense of the gargantuan chasm that must be spanned to legitimately claim that patient perspectives are being acknowledged, identified, and honoured. The terms "overuse", "underuse", and "misuse", for example, are construed from the perspective of the service *provider,* not the service consumer. That is, what is currently being considered is the way in which health professionals over- or under*treat,* not necessarily the extent to which the services are being over- or under*used* by patients. This is not a trivial issue. The extent to which patients follow medication protocols as prescribed by their treating physicians can range from 0% to 100% with an average of approximately 50% (Nieuwlaat et al., 2014). When rates of medication in a population are being discussed, therefore, it is extremely important to be clear about whether one is referring to medication *prescribing* or medication *consumption* because these are not the same thing (Carey and Salter, 2017).

Accepting the centrality of patients' preferences and values also has implications for the concept of the grey zone which has just been discussed. The concept of the grey zone is presented in terms of a continuum of the net effect of services with clearly ineffective services at one end and clearly effective services at the other (Brownlee et al., 2017). The grey zone lies in between these two extremes. A service, however, is an inert procedure or substance. It is the *interaction* between the service and the patient which creates an outcome that lies on the continuum from clearly ineffective to clearly effective. Brownlee et al. (2017, p. 1) hint at the importance of this interaction when they define effective services as "tests and treatments that are universally beneficial when used *on the appropriate patient*" [emphasis added]. So a test or treatment is not universally beneficial per se. Beneficial tests or treatments are beneficial *when used on the appropriate patient*. Gotzsche (2013) points out that drugs always cause harm and that, for all drugs, it is essential to find the dose that causes more good than harm for most patients.

The continuum proposed by Brownlee et al. (2017), therefore, is, ultimately a continuum of the interaction between procedures and products and the patients who use them. Even the notion of an effective or ineffective service cannot be divorced from the patient's preferences and values. The patient, for example, is the best judge of whether a subjective effect of a drug outweighs its side effects (Gotzsche, 2015). An antidepressant may improve a patient's mood, but if it also introduces akathisia and weight gain, this may not be deemed an effective treatment by the patient. Unfortunately, too often, it can be the case that the patients' complaints about side effects are ignored, and they are compelled to continue taking medications that they find unpleasant (Gotzsche, 2015).

The patient's perspective, therefore, is pivotal to the provision of appropriate care or the right health care. There is a great deal more that can be done, however, to position the patient's perspective as the driving force in health care. The remainder of this book advances the idea of patient-perspective care as a paradigm shift in health care generally and mental health specifically. Currently, "patient-centred" care is the dominant manifesto in health service provision, yet patient-centred care has strayed from its initial position and, ironically, has failed to place patient priorities as the centrepiece of decision making in health.

In the chapters ahead . . .

In the next chapter, I will explain a little more closely some of the factors that might have been responsible for getting us to where we are at the moment. Then I will present some of the evidence, both implicit and explicit, in the literature, that demonstrates the failure of the patient-centred approach – or at least our failure to fully embrace its original intent. Showing that the patient-centred approach has failed is not enough, necessarily, to justify changing to a patient-perspective paradigm, so in Chapter 4, I will spend some more time demonstrating the importance of the perspective of the patient. Any new initiative should be informed by robust theoretical principles. Perhaps the lack of a solid theoretical foundation is one of the reasons that the patient-centred approach has failed as completely as it has. I will outline Perceptual Control Theory (PCT) as a compelling justification for the necessity of the patient-perspective movement. Much of our current literature is occupied by debates and quibbles about issues such as objectivity, subjectivity, and the nature of reality. The position of PCT is that we are living *subjectively* in an *objective*, physical world. From this theoretical basis, I will outline in general terms some of the practical implications for a patient-perspective attitude to health care. Next I will describe a specific example of the redesign of one aspect of health care service provision according to patient-perspective ideals. The impact of this new way of working on waiting times, missed appointments, and referral capacity is discussed. A book about a patient-perspective approach to health care would be incomplete without including actual patients' perspectives, so Chapter 8 provides the experiences of some people in their roles as patients or consumers of health services. The final chapter considers the kinds of changes in education and training, policy development, and public education initiatives that will be required for the patient-perspective paradigm to pervasively penetrate health systems and services.

The patient-perspective approach is an opportunity for health care provision generally, although my background is in clinical psychology, so at times, the examples and illustrations may have a strong mental health flavour. More than anything, however, it is the principles of patient-perspective care that are important rather than the particular ways this mindset might manifest in any specific health care context. The final blueprint for how a patient-perspective approach will be realised in all health settings is far from established. Perhaps, as you read through these pages, you will develop your own strategies about the most ideal way of applying these principles in the health setting within which you work. I'll look forward to hearing about your progress in adopting this attitude to the fundamentally important task of helping people achieve their ideal health and well-being.

References

Berwick, D. M., & Hackbarth, A. D. (2012). Eliminating waste in US health care. *JAMA*, *307*, 1513–1516.

Blank, T., Graves, K., Sepucha, K., & Llewellyn-Thomas, H. (2006). Understanding treatment decision making: Contexts, commonalities, complexities, and challenges. *Annals of Behavioral Medicine*, *32*, 211–217.

Brownlee, S., Chalkidou, K., Doust, J., Elshaug, A. G., Glasziou, P., Heath, I., . . . Korenstein, D. (2017). Evidence for overuse of medical services around the world. *Lancet*, Published online 8 January. http://dx.doi.org/10.1016/S0140-6736(16)32585-5

Carey, T. A., & Salter, A. (2017). Links between antidepressants and suicide and homicide: Commentary on Bouvy and Liem (2012). *Ethical Human Psychology and Psychiatry*, *18*(3), 258–262.

Chassin, M. R., & Galvin, R. W. (1998). The urgent need to improve health care quality. Institute of Medicine National Roundtable on Health Care Quality. *JAMA*, *280*, 1000–1005.

Gotzsche, P. (2013). *Deadly medicines and organised crime: How big pharma has corrupted healthcare*. London: Radcliffe Publishing.

Gotzsche, P. (2015). *Deadly psychiatry and organised denial*. Copenhagen: People's Press.

Nieuwlaat, R., Wilczynski, N., Navarro, T., Hobson, N., Jeffery, R., . . . Haynes, R. B. (2014). Interventions for enhancing medication adherence. *Cochrane Database of Systematic Reviews*, Issue 11 (Art. No.: CD000011). doi:10.1002/14651858.CD000011.pub4

Saini, V., Brownlee, S., Elshaug, A. G., Glasziou, P., & Heath, I. (2017). Addressing overuse and underuse around the world. *Lancet*, Published online 8 January. http://dx.doi.org/10.1016/S0140-6736(16)32573-9

2

HOW HAVE WE ARRIVED AT THIS POSITION?

It is useful to spend time considering some of the factors that may have steered us to the current situation in which inappropriate health care is commonplace instead of being a rare phenomenon. Understanding these forces might help to ensure that similar mistakes are not repeated when attempts are made to correct the problem. There has undoubtedly been a multiplicity of contributing influences, but one factor in particular that has profoundly affected our beliefs and practices has been our allegiance to Western biomedical science. The conceptualisation of disease as the disruption of biological variables or the deviation of these variables away from the specified "normal" state has led to a myriad of startling successes such as antibiotics, vaccines, and organ transplantation. We are living in an age of unprecedented cleverness when procedures that people would have been considered foolhardy to even dream of a few decades ago are now routine.

The downside to the biomedical model

Our ingenuity, however, has come at a price. In many ways, the scientific enterprise has come to be cherished above all else with a consequent preponderance of reductionist thinking and the lure of the commercial imperatives of product development driving suboptimal care in many cases (Saini, Garcia-Armesto et al., 2017). While it might be expected that biomedical research would be asking and answering questions that are important to patients, it appears that approximately 85% of the funding globally is wasted on research that fails in this regard (Saini, Garcia-Armesto et al., 2017). Saini, Garcia-Armesto et al. (2017) cite numerous reasons for this failure such as study endpoints that are chosen by professionals but not important to patients, adverse reactions and long-term outcomes being disregarded, and short-term successes with newsworthy results being favoured over outcomes that are meaningful to health.

Somewhere along the way, we seem to have lost sight of the fact that the biomedical model of health and wellness is a necessary but not sufficient aspect of the appropriate care of patients (Saini, Garcia-Armesto et al., 2017). Gotzsche (2015) reminds us that evidence-based health care should rest on three pillars: reliable research, clinical expertise, and the patient's values and preferences. Currently, however, research exists along all possible points of a continuum of reliability and clinical expertise which is subject to the vagaries of health professionals' perceptual biases and heuristics are the two driving forces in health care decision making. The component representing patient's values and preferences is, in no way, on an equal footing with the other two elements. Even if we could restore the balance to three equal pillars, we would still have room to improve. Reliable research and clinical expertise need to be used *in the service of* patient's values and preferences.

Research must be about the things that are of most concern to the people who will be the ultimate beneficiaries of the results of the research. Currently, some research seems to benefit the careers of the researchers in terms of attracting grants and producing publications more than it assists patients to live the lives they wish for themselves. Similarly, clinical expertise must be driven by the issues that patients want to have addressed.

It is the needs and informed priorities and preferences of patients that must define what desirable outcomes are and what appropriate care is (Saini, Garcia-Armesto et al., 2017). We need to keep at the front of our minds that less than 20% of a populations' health status is brought about by its health care delivery systems (Saini, Garcia-Armesto et al., 2017). The biomedical model, however, has become somewhat of a master. We have lost sight of the fact that it is a model only. And as far as scientific standards are concerned, it is not even a very outstanding model. As will be explained in Chapter 5, the model fails in crucial ways because it is an inaccurate depiction of human functioning.

Somewhere along the way, we have mistaken what is *possible* for what is *necessary*. In the ideal and tightly controlled context of the research environment, we have been able to demonstrate the outcomes that are possible with certain doses and durations of treatment. In the context of people's lives, however, only the individuals themselves know the benefits that are necessary so that they can experience day-to-day living the way they want.

The misuse of norms

Our subservience to the biomedical model has resulted in an almost exclusive focus on correcting deviations from biological norms instead of helping patients meet important needs. Part of the problem here is that many of the biological norms we have established are essentially arbitrary. These norms do not specify the physiological and biochemical states that are necessary to live contented and productive lives. Definitions of "normal" bone density or "normal" cholesterol are good examples of this

(Moynihan and Cassels, 2005). Related to a rigid fixation with concepts of normality are the "pre-" conditions that have been created more recently. Prehypertension and prediabetes are two such instances (Gotzsche, 2013).

Saini, Garcia-Armesto et al. (2017) indicate that our allegiance to this biomedical model is one of the important factors contributing to what they describe as a "widespread lack of patient involvement in decisions and treatment goals" (p. 5). Patients' goals can often take time to discover; however, health professionals should never assume that the goals are missing or otherwise non-existent. Nor should health professionals assume that the patients' goals are the same as their own.

By focusing on norms created by the health industry instead of the goals of people accessing the resources of this industry, we have developed an almost exclusive focus on medical interventions and a relative neglect for other approaches such as counselling and behavioural therapies or preventative approaches including social and public health initiatives (Saini, Garcia-Armesto et al., 2017). In many cases, we emphasise treatments over lifestyle factors such as diet and exercise. Moreover, we have lost sight of the fact that health care provision should be a means to an end, not the end in itself. The end is to help patients realise the goals that are important to them (Saini, Garcia-Armesto et al., 2017). Through this chronic goal neglect, we have come to overuse treatments such as chemotherapy in cases of advanced cancer (Saini, Garcia-Armesto et al., 2017).

Acknowledging the impact of the power imbalance

Despite the conceptual difficulties of the grey zone mentioned earlier, it is precisely because there are uncertainty and variability in the benefits and harms of many of our treatments that the goals, perspectives, and preferences of patients must be taken so seriously. Saini, Brownlee et al. (2017) maintain that "The medical community needs to do what patients want rather than what health professionals know how to do" (p. 1). The simplicity and directness of this statement belies how difficult it can be in clinical practice to elicit patient's goals. The factors discussed so far in this chapter, such as the establishment of arbitrary norms and research that benefits researchers more than patients, are some of the aspects of the health care system that strongly indicate that there is frequently a very significant power imbalance between the health professional and the patient. This means that patients might not always be frank and forthcoming about the things that are genuinely important to them. Rather, they may defer to the presumed wisdom of their treating health professional. Or they may guess at what they believe the health professional would want them to do and say rather than what they would actually like to say and do.

In moving towards an era of health care when patient perspectives authentically steer service provision, the power imbalance may be one of the first issues to address. Saini, Brownlee et al. (2017) propose that central to understanding poor health care is having some appreciation of the crucial underlying disparities in information, wealth, and power. There is no doubt that we could be doing better at educating and activating the public. Too much trust and faith are apportioned to the literature that is churned out of the health industry. A great deal of this information is designed to maximise the profits for the company producing the documents. People need to learn to become as sceptical of health information as they might be about shampoo or car advertisements. Part of the social responsibility of health professionals to patients specifically and the public more generally is to provide assistance and support in questioning the available information to come to conclusions that will be most appropriate for them given their context and the lives they are fashioning for themselves.

Even when patients are not able to directly express their particular perspectives with regard to the health issue being discussed, it is often possible to develop an appreciation of their stances by the way in which they respond. In this sense, even though dissenting patients can be bothersome to a busy and frazzled health professional, they can also provide valuable information by their dissent about where their priorities might lie. Do they seem reluctant or hesitant to adopt the protocol that you're recommending? Do they not follow their medication regimen as specified? Do they miss appointments? All of these responses can be indicators of hidden but important goals and values that are having a powerful influence on the way in which a patient uses the resources of the health service. Rather than labelling patients as non-compliant and implementing strategies to correct their non-compliant ways, it would be more beneficial to seek first to understand the effect of the apparent non-compliance for these patients. What is the non-compliance achieving or maintaining for them? Are there important aspects of their lives that would be disrupted if they diligently complied with the advice and instructions of the health professional? Answers to questions such as these may provide some important insights regarding how best to proceed with the provision of services that are useful to patients from their perspective.

The place at which we have arrived

Through a myriad of twists and turns, we now find ourselves in a situation in which inappropriate health care by the overuse or underuse of indices and interventions is rampant. The dazzling success of Western biomedical science has blinded us from looking more closely at the extent to which our tests and treatments are helping or hindering the patients we serve. The rise of the patient-centred ethos may have been an attempt to push the pendulum in the opposite direction, but in ways that will be explained in the next chapter, this has also failed. A dramatic reorganisation is required, and the patient-perspective paradigm is the means to bring this about. A necessary component of adopting this new way of approaching health care service provision will be to convince patients that their perspectives are legitimate and that they have every right to express them and pursue them.

Patient-centred health care has failed, and it is imperative that a new age of health care begins in which the cornerstone of appropriate care is the perspective of the patient. The next chapter will provide evidence of the failure of the patient-centred attitude, and the subsequent chapter will demonstrate why it is that the patient-perspective paradigm is so important. The continued harm to patients through the overuse or underuse of health care services as well as the ongoing waste of precious and limited financial resources must end. To move away from the position we now find ourselves in, we need a different approach, a novel way of considering health care service provision as well as the patients who access our expertise. The patient-perspective paradigm is the vehicle we need to complete that quest.

References

Gotzsche, P. (2013). *Deadly medicines and organised crime: How big pharma has corrupted healthcare*. London: Radcliffe Publishing.

Gotzsche, P. (2015). *Deadly psychiatry and organised denial*. Copenhagen: People's Press.

Moynihan, R., & Cassels, A. (2005). *Selling sickness: How the world's biggest pharmaceutical companies are turning us all into patients*. New York: Nation Books.

Saini, V., Brownlee, S., Elshaug, A. G., Glasziou, P., & Heath, I. (2017). Addressing overuse and underuse around the world. *Lancet*, Published online 8 January. http://dx.doi.org/10.1016/S0140-6736(16)32573-9

Saini, V., Garcia-Armesto, S., Klemperer, D., Paris, V., Elshaug, A. G., Brownlee, S., . . . Fisher, E. S. (2017). Drivers of poor medical care. *Lancet*, Published online 8 January. http://dx.doi.org/10.1016/S0140-6736(16)30947-3

3

WHY HAS THE CONCEPT OF PATIENT-CENTRED CARE FAILED?

The evidence that the concept of patient-centred care has failed to be applied as intended in routine clinical practice is provided both implicitly and explicitly in the literature and is extensive. References to patient-centred care in the literature can be traced back to the 1950s, although there is still no universally agreed definition of the term (Carey, 2016). The Institute of Medicine (2014) defines patient-centred care as "providing care that is respectful of and responsive to individual patient preferences, needs, and values, and ensuring that patient values guide all clinical decisions" (p. 6). This definition strongly resonates with the patient-perspective ethos; however, it appears that it has been devilishly difficult to embody this definition in practice.

There are certainly isolated practices and services that are attempting to correct the inadequacies of the patient-centred approach. For example, "patient-driven" health care is described as a current priority in the US Department of Veterans Affairs. In this system, health care is driven by the things that matter to the patient (Krejci, Carter and Gaudet, 2014). This is entirely consistent with the patient-perspective approach, but the fact that it is described as "patient driven" rather than "patient centred" is an indication that the patient-centred term is, in some ways, unsuitable for the system of care this particular organisation wants to implement.

Perspective, not position

Perhaps it is the spatial emphasis in the term "patient centred" that creates some of the difficulty, by allowing health professionals to keep patients at the *centre* of their deliberations while also providing these health professionals with scope to legitimately ignore patient preferences *and* still subscribe to a patient-centred model. McCance, McCormack and Dewing (2011), for example, argue that patient-centred care requires placing the patient at the centre of care delivery. Where a patient is placed, however, is merely geography. Emphasising the centre, versus any other position, as the appropriate position for the patient to be situated does not highlight the imperative for health care decisions to be driven by patient preferences. The patient-perspective approach, on the other, emphasises *perspective* rather than *position*.

A comment on language

The failure of the patient-centred approach is demonstrated no more clearly than by particular words and terms that have become part of the everyday vernacular of many health professionals. It is not at all unusual, for example, to describe people who do not follow their treating health professional's advice as "non-compliant" or people who do not improve with a given course of treatment as "treatment resistant". Similarly, it has been identified for almost two decades that people who do not attend as many sessions of psychological treatment as their clinician thinks they should attend are often referred to as "treatment dropouts" (Mueller and Pekarik, 2000) even though these people may have achieved the results they wanted.

A long-standing disconnect

In fact, there is a significant and long-standing disconnect between the number of sessions psychological treatments are designed to be by clinicians and researchers and the number of sessions patients typically access in routine clinical practice (Carey and Spratt, 2009; Carey, Tai, Mansell, Huddy, Griffiths and Marken, 2017). Whereas most treatments are designed to be more than ten sessions, people accessing treatments typically attend an average of four to six sessions. Moreover, while most clinicians prefer to schedule regular treatment sessions at weekly or fortnightly intervals, many patients prefer to attend a variable schedule of treatment sessions as evidenced by the missed and cancelled appointments that are a regular and costly feature of health care service provision. Treatments, therefore, are not currently designed from the patient's perspective nor are they delivered from the patient's perspective.

The fracture that exists between practitioners' and patients' expectations regarding the duration of psychological treatments has created a staggering amount of waste. Obviously, if a treatment is designed to be 12 sessions and a person attends only four of these sessions *and makes the changes she wants to make*, then, clearly, eight entire sessions were unnecessary for this person. Yet because of the current climate, the clinician may feel compelled to "encourage" the person to attend for all 12 sessions and equally likely to consider the person a "treatment dropout" when she stops coming after four sessions. With a patient-perspective approach, treatment is provided within the patient's timeframe rather than the clinician's for a more efficient and effective service. In fact, even the definition of what constitutes an effective treatment would be determined by the patient rather than the clinician. More will be said about structuring the delivery of treatments from the patient's perspective in Chapter 7.

Problems with our research methodology

Currently, our dominant research methodology, many of our treatment guidelines, and even our diagnostic systems all minimise the patient's perspective. By far, the dominant methodology in health care at the moment for developing and delivering treatments is the randomised controlled trial (RCT; Carey and Stiles, 2016). The RCT is a sophisticated and powerful research tool; however, it has been inappropriately applied in many, but certainly not all, cases in terms of finding ways to address health problems effectively and efficiently. A detailed analysis of the RCT is beyond the scope of this book; however, it is relevant to note that the RCT makes a very clear statement about causality. In fact, the purpose of the highly controlled procedures of the RCT is so that inferences about causality can be made. And with an RCT, it is assumed it is the treatment that creates the effects in the people receiving the treatment (Carey and Stiles, 2016). This might be a defensible assumption to a certain extent if one is considering a surgical procedure or a pharmacological treatment, but the assumption becomes untenable when used in the context of psychological treatments. Patients are not inert objects that are shaped and modified by powerful treatments. A patient who engages in a programme of psychological treatment interacts with the therapist, and the treatment is modified as it is delivered according to how the patient responds. The attitude of considering patients as active decision makers during the treatment process has been called "responsive regulation" (Stiles, Barkham, Connell, and Mellor-Clark, 2008), but the idea of patients as responsive regulators is still barely recognised in health care.

Another problem with RCTs relates to the schism mentioned earlier between how long researchers and clinicians think treatments *should be* and how long patients *want* them to be as evidenced by their attendance patterns. To conduct an RCT, a treatment is packaged into a standardised protocol of a pre-determined number of sessions. Suppose a 12-session treatment is developed. The general procedure is then to recruit a group of people and to provide the treatment to half the group. The group that gets the treatment and the group that doesn't get it are randomly determined. After the treatment has been administered, if the average outcome of the treatment group is better than the average outcome of the other group, according to some established benchmark, it is considered appropriate to conclude that the 12-session treatment is an effective treatment. Research such as this, however, is a fine example of the way in which we have conflated what is *possible* and what is *necessary*. A study such as the one that has been described has certainly demonstrated that it is *possible* to effectively assist people with the amelioration of whatever problem the treatment was designed to address by offering 12 sessions of the treatment. A study such as this, however, is *not* a demonstration that 12 sessions are *necessary* to address the problem (Carey and Spratt, 2009; Carey et al., 2017). This distinction between what is *possible* and what is *necessary* is crucial, but it is a distinction that has been missed by many people, including policymakers who develop guidelines for treatment delivery. It is certainly admirable to develop standards of best practice, but here again, it is critical to remember that what is "best" from a health care provider's perspective will not always be "best" from the patient's perspective.

Randomised controlled trials require that treatments are standardised across patients and clinicians, which results in treatments of fixed durations. Even when these treatments are brief, the fact that they are a pre-determined number of sessions means that they will not be the right number of sessions for all patients.

Meuldijk et al. (2015), for example, describe a treatment they call "concise care" which has a fixed number of weekly sessions with a maximum of seven sessions and is delivered within a seven-week fixed time period after which time the concise care ends. Given that this treatment is predetermined regardless of a patient's individual circumstances and problems, it is hard to understand the sense in which it is considered "care". At least, providing a particular treatment to a patient irrespective of that patient's values and preferences would not be considered care within a patient-perspective system of health care.

In the United Kingdom, the National Institute for Health and Clinical Excellence (NICE) recommend that, "For all people with depression having individual CBT [cognitive behaviour therapy], the duration of treatment should typically be in the range of 16 to 20 sessions over three to four months" (NICE, 2009, p. 27). It is easy to understand how guidelines like this could have been developed when RCTs are still mistakenly regarded as the "gold standard" of evidence in health care (Carey and Stiles, 2016). A naïve consideration of the empirical evidence might appear to suggest that the recommendation of 16 to 20 sessions is what the research results across many RCTs demonstrate. The study of how many sessions are *necessary* for patients to use treatments effectively, however, has not yet been conducted. Guidelines such as the NICE suggestions for the treatment of depression, therefore, provide strong evidence of service overuse in which patients will be prompted to attend far more sessions than the number of sessions most patients will need or want. The evidence from routine clinical practice indicates that, generally, with regard to psychological treatments, a large number of patients require a small number of sessions, and a small number of patients require a large number of sessions (Carey and Spratt, 2009). This evidence would be easily accommodated within a patient-perspective approach but is currently ignored in our current era of patient-centred care.

Problems with the use of guidelines

Guidelines in other areas of health care also suggest the overuse of services by encouraging overdiagnosis. The consequent medical intervention is then administered without any clear benefit to the patient, from the patient's perspective, in many cases. Brownlee et al. (2017) describe a review of guidelines in the USA in which ten of the 16 guidelines had been widened sufficiently to allow the potential for overuse. By lowering the risk thresholds for treating cholesterol, for example, prescriptions of lipid-lowering medication are being dispensed to increasing proportions of populations in many countries without clear indicators of benefit (Brownlee et al., 2017). In children, overdiagnosis is also a concern with purported disorders such as attention deficient hyperactivity disorder (ADHD), food allergies, and gastroesophageal reflux being identified too frequently in many cases (Brownlee et al., 2017, p. 4).

A fine example of the disconnect I have been referring to was produced during the evaluation of the first year of the Improving Accessing to Psychological Therapies (IAPT) in the United Kingdom (Glover, Webb, and Evison, 2010). Bearing in mind that the NICE guidelines referred to previously applied to the services involved in this evaluation, Glover et al. reported that the "numbers of treatment sessions were surprisingly low" (p. 23). The reason these numbers were "surprising" is, perhaps, because of an erroneous expectation established by the NICE guidelines. Of the 7,825 patients providing data, only 1.38% of them attended 16 or more treatment sessions. The median number of appointments was less than ten (Glover et al. 2010). This median number of appointments is entirely consistent with what is found in routine clinical practice (Carey, 2011), so this average should not have been surprising at all. Clearly, we need treatments that are designed and delivered according to patients' perspectives of appropriate time frames. The patient–perspective imperative is also relevant when the way in which patient problems are conceptualised.

Diagnosis can contribute to the problem of inappropriate care

With regard to psychological problems and understanding the nature of a person's psychological distress, the fifth edition of the *Diagnostic and Statistical Manual of Mental Disorders* (DSM-5; American Psychiatric Association (APA), 2013) is highly problematic. Fried and Nesse (2015) analysed the symptom profiles of 3703 patients seeking treatment for major depressive disorder (MDD) who were recruited to the STAR*D trial. From these 3,703 patients, 1,030 unique symptom profiles were identified with 501 profiles identified by only one individual each. Fried and Nesse (2015) suggest that this substantial heterogeneity calls into question the status of MDD as a specific consistent syndrome. At the very least, grouping together people with different symptom profiles under the one diagnostic heading ignores the value of each patient's perspective of their difficulties.

A large amount of symptom variability captured under one diagnostic label is not peculiar to MDD but is a general characteristic of the DSM nosology. With post-traumatic stress disorder, for example, it has been calculated that 175 different symptom combinations all qualify for the diagnosis (Lareau, 2012). Even more startling is conduct disorder. Because of the way in which the criteria are grouped for this diagnostic category, as well as the rules that specify which symptoms and how many from each grouping are necessary, 32,647 different symptom patterns all qualify for a diagnosis of conduct disorder (Perepletchikova and Kazdin, 2005).

Collecting the experiences and troubles of different people under one diagnostic label is particularly pernicious because it conveys a sense of understanding but actually obscures the very clarity it pretends to portray. A health professional might, after obtaining information from a patient, inform the patient that he has conduct disorder, or MDD, or some other diagnostic label.

The label, however, is nothing more than a summary term for the difficulties the patient has just described to the health professional. Superficially, it appears to explain the person's troubles in the same way that a diagnosis of diabetes might help a person understand why he is experiencing things such as fatigue, increased thirst, and frequent urination. Actually, though, a DSM diagnosis is devoid of this kind of explanatory power. Moreover, when health professionals such as a general practitioner (GP) and a clinical psychologist communicate with each other about a patient with whom they are jointly working, the clinical psychologist might suggest to the GP that the patient "has" MDD. As explained earlier, it has been demonstrated empirically that this unitary label can be applied to a vast number of different symptom profiles (Fried and Nesse, 2015), so by providing the GP with the label rather than a summary of the patient's problems, the clinical psychologist is, in fact, limiting, rather than enhancing, the GP's insight into the patient's situation. Upon hearing this diagnosis, the GP might mistakenly believe she now understands the nature of the person's difficulties, which could lead her to make assumptions about the person rather than seeking to understand, from the patient, the troubles with which the patient is currently contending.

Who decides?

A failure to consider the patient's perspective, therefore, can be identified in research, policy, practice, and diagnostic contexts. Given this situation, it is perhaps not surprising that many clinicians find it difficult to incorporate the patient's perspective into their health care planning. Saini, Garcia-Armesto et al. (2017) emphasise this point. They describe the involvement of patients in treatment decisions as an ethical imperative but list factors such as time, clinician resistance, and systemic constraints as barriers to genuine and meaningful patient involvement. It appears that deciding what is in another person's best interests has become commonplace in health care service provision. My stance in this book is that there is not only an ethical imperative to adopt a patient–perspective approach in health care but there are also moral, financial, and societal imperatives. Deciding what is best for another person from the position of providing health treatments can lead to the unnecessary harm of the person; the imprudent use of finite, and often expensive resources; and a failure of communities and societies to be as productive and cohesive as they otherwise might be.

A closer look at the idea of shared decision making

Currently, despite patient-centred care being an oft repeated slogan, patients are rarely involved in a shared decision making process (Saini, Garcia-Armesto et al., 2017). This tendency to keep patients at the centre of deliberations while excluding them from involvement in decisions that matter to them appears to occur even with elective surgery. Saini, Garcia-Armesto et al. (2017) report that RCTs repeatedly demonstrate that an average of 20% of elective treatment procedures would not be agreed to by patients if they were able to access clinical information that was relevant and understandable to them. Current decision-making processes, therefore, which ignore the patient's perspective, are driving the inappropriate administration of health care services (Saini, Garcia-Armesto et al., 2017).

Even the concept of shared decision making, however, reveals the limitations of the patient-centred model. Given that health care is one of the means by which patients can be enabled to continue pursuing goals that are important to them, it is unlikely that "shared decision making" is ever an appropriate model. Health professionals will not *share* the life goals of the patients to whom they provide services, so it is difficult to understand the sense in which decision making should be shared. If the perspective of the patient is genuinely regarded as the key to effective decision making, then a model of *supported*, rather than *shared*, decision making should be sought (Carey, 2016). A supported decision making model would require that patients' decisions were the main item on the agenda in a way that the concept of shared decision making does not.

A clash between policy and practice

Empirical evidence of the failure to realise the ideals of the patient-centred approach can sometimes indicate a clash between policy directives and the practicalities of clinical practice. Bower, Gilbody, and Barkham (2006), for example, acknowledged government policies that emphasise the importance of patient choice. They suggest, however, that promoting patient choice in service delivery is problematic because of the differences between the population and the individual perspectives (Bower et al. 2006). The clash between the individual and the population perspectives was highlighted by Kilfedder et al. (2010) in their study comparing three different psychological treatments. In the RCT they conducted, they found that bibliotherapy, telephone counselling, and face-to-face counselling were all equally effective and that patients preferred face-to-face counselling rather than bibliotherapy or telephone counselling. Remarkably, however, in their conclusions, Kilfedder et al. (2010) recommended that *bibliotherapy* should be offered first to patients in a stepped care model because it is the least costly of the three approaches. Although bibliotherapy might be more financially attractive in the short term, offering patients treatments that are unsatisfactory from their perspective can lead to increased costs at a later date. Almost 20 years ago, for example, Breslin et al. (1998) suggested that if patients are offered treatment that they consider to be less than what they need, they will be likely to seek out greater care in other settings.

The IAPT model mentioned earlier is a large-scale stepped care service implemented throughout England and Wales. While the provision of services of different intensity would appear to promote patient choice, it seems that this is not the case with IAPT. Binnie (2015), for example, reported that working collaboratively with patients is not an approach that is widely used in IAPT services. As with other systems of care, patient centeredness is promoted in IAPT, although the rigidity of services and an inability to manage individual needs and preferences have been described as major barriers to attendance (Marshall et al., 2015); McQueen and Smith (2015) also reported that the stepped care model deprives patients of individualised treatment and choice. In an RCT of stepped care for the treatment of bulimia nervosa, Mitchell et al. (2011) reported that their results suggest that treatment is enhanced with an individualised approach. The fact that individualising treatment is still considered noteworthy enough to mention in a 2011 research publication is a clear demonstration of how typical it has become to ignore patient's perspectives and offer standardised treatments to patients who only ever have idiosyncratic problems.

In summary

In numerous ways, therefore, it is evident that the patient-centred approach to health care service provision has failed. Adopting a patient-perspective attitude is urgently required. Considering the choice between patient-centred and patient-perspective health care is not simply a question of different flavours but actually demands a commitment to adopt a fundamentally different approach to service provision that has important implications for the efficient and effective delivery of procedures and protocols.

References

American Psychiatric Association (APA). (2013). *Diagnostic and statistical manual of mental disorders* (5th ed.). Washington, DC: Author.

Binnie, J. (2015). Do you want therapy with that? A critical account of working within IAPT. *Mental Health Review Journal, 20*(2), 79–83.

Bower, P., Gilbody, S., & Barkham, M. (2006). Making decisions about patient progress: The application of routine outcome measurement in stepped care psychological therapy services. *Primary Care Mental Health, 4*(1), 21–28.

Brownlee, S., Chalkidou, K., Doust, J., Elshaug, A. G., Glasziou, P., Heath, I., . . . Korenstein, D. (2017). Evidence for overuse of medical services around the world. *Lancet*, Published online 8 January. http://dx.doi.org/10.1016/S0140-6736(16)32585-5

Carey, T. A. (2011). As you like it: Adopting a patient-led approach to psychological treatments. *Journal of Public Mental Health, 10*(1), 6–16.

Carey, T. A. (2016). Beyond patient-centred care: Enhancing the patient experience in mental health services through patient-perspective care. *Patient Experience Journal, 3*(2), 46–49.

Carey, T. A., & Spratt, M. B. (2009). When is enough enough? Structuring the organization of treatment to maximise patient choice and control. *The Cognitive Behaviour Therapist, 2*, 211–226.

Carey, T. A., & Stiles, W. B. (2016). Some problems with randomized controlled trials and some viable alternatives. *Clinical Psychology & Psychotherapy, 23*(1), 87–95. doi:10.1002/cpp.1942

Carey, T. A., Tai, S. J., Mansell, W., Huddy, V., Griffiths, R., & Marken, R. S. (2017). Improving professional psychological practice through an increased repertoire of research methodologies: Illustrated by the development of MOL. *Professional Psychology: Research and Practice.* Advance online publication. http://dx.doi.org/10.1037/pro0000132

Fried, E. I., & Nesse, R. M. (2015). Depression is not a consistent syndrome: An investigation of unique symptom patterns in the STAR_D study. *Journal of Affective Disorders, 172*, 96–102. http://dx.doi.org/10.1016/j.jad.2014.10.010

Glover, G., Webb, M., & Evison, F. (2010). *Improving access to psychological therapies: A review of the progress made by sites in the first roll-out year.* Stockton-on-Tees, UK: North East Public Health Observatory.

Institute of Medicine. (2014). *Crossing the quality chasm: A new health system for the 21st century.* Washington, DC: National Academy Press. Retrieved April 14, 2017, from www.nap.edu/openbook.php?record_id=10027&page=R1

Kilfedder, C., Power, K., Karatzias, T., McCafferty, A., Niven, K., Chouliara, Z., Galloway, L., & Sharp, S. (2010). A randomized trial of face-to-face counselling versus telephone counselling versus bibliotherapy for occupational stress. *Psychology and Psychotherapy: Theory, Research and Practice, 83*(3), 223–242.

Krejci, L. P., Carter, K., & Gaudet, T. (2014). The vision and implementation of personalized, proactive, patient driven health care for Veterans. *Medical Care, 52*(12 Suppl 5), S5–S8.

Lareau, C. R. (2012). Posttraumatic stress disorder and acute stress disorder. In D. Faust (Ed.), *Coping with psychiatric and psychological testimony* (pp. 610–635). Oxford: Oxford University Press.

Marshall, D., Quinn, C., Child, S., Shenton, D., Pooler, J., Forber, S., & Byng, R. (2015). What IAPT services can learn from those who do not attend. *Journal of Mental Health, 25*(5), 410–415.

McCance, T., McCormack, B., & Dewing, J. (2011). An exploration of person-centredness in practice. *Online Journal of Issues in Nursing, 16*(2). doi:10.3912/OJIN.Vol16No02Man01

McQueen, D., & Smith, P. St. J. (2015). NICE recommendations for psychotherapy in depression: Of limited clinical utility. *Psychiatriki, 26*(3), 188–197.

Meuldijk, D., Carlier, I. V. E., van Vliet, I. M., van Hemert, A. M., Zitman, F. G., & van den Akker-van Marle, M. E. (2015). Economic evaluation of concise cognitive behavioural therapy and/or pharmacotherapy for depressive and anxiety disorders. *Journal of Mental Health Policy and Economics, 18*(4), 175–183.

Mitchell, J. E., Agras, S., Crow, S., Halmi, K., Fairburn, C. G., Bryson, S., & Kraemer, H. (2011). Stepped care and cognitive-behavioural therapy for bulimia nervosa: Randomised trial. *British Journal of Psychiatry, 198*(5), 391–397.

Mueller, M., & Pekarik, G. (2000). Treatment duration prediction: Client accuracy, and its relationship to dropout, outcome, and satisfaction. *Psychotherapy, 37*, 117–123.

NICE. (2009). *Depression: The treatment and management of depression in adults.* London, UK: National Institute for Health and Clinical Excellence. Retrieved June 27, 2017, from nice.org.uk/guidance/cg90

Perepletchikova, F., & Kazdin, A. E. (2005). Oppositional defiant disorder and conduct disorder. In K. Cheng and K. M. Myers (Eds.), *Child and adolescent psychiatry: The essentials* (pp. 73–88). Philadelphia, PA: Lippincott Williams & Wilkins.

Saini, V., Garcia-Armesto, S., Klemperer, D., Paris, V., Elshaug, A. G., Brownlee, S., . . . Fisher, E. S. (2017). Drivers of poor medical care. *Lancet*, Published online 8 January. http://dx.doi.org/10.1016/S0140-6736(16)30947-3

Stiles, W. B., Barkham, M., Connell, J., & Mellor-Clark, J. (2008). Responsive regulation of treatment duration in routine practice in United Kingdom primary care settings: Replication in a larger sample. *Journal of Consulting and Clinical Psychology, 76*(2), 298–305.

4

THE IMPORTANCE OF THE PATIENT'S PERSPECTIVE

Inappropriate care is the scourge of efficient and effective health services. How to provide health care more appropriately appears to be an intractable problem for many health systems. Perhaps the widespread failure to recognise that the extent to which care is appropriate or inappropriate is determined by the patient receiving the care is a large part of the problem. In the final analysis, "help" can only be defined by the recipient, rather than the provider, of the help. Ultimately, health care entails supporting individuals to achieve and maintain the necessary physical and psychological states to realise the goals they have for themselves in terms of creating the lives they would like to live. To provide appropriate health care, therefore, it is important to understand the goals of patients accessing the service as well as having some appreciation of the lives they would like to be living. It should not be assumed that the life a patient would like to be living will be the same as the life the treating health professional likes to live or the life the treating health professional thinks the patient *should* be living.

An illustration in the area of quality of life

A striking example of the importance of the patient's perspective was provided in a deceptively simple study conducted more than 25 years ago by Jachuck and colleagues. The study was an investigation of the effect of hypotensive medication on a patient's quality of life. Included in the study were 75 consecutive patients (41 women and 34 men) from one group practice who all had controlled hypertension. Data were collected from these patients as well as from a close companion of each patient and the patients' GPs. The patients, close companions, and GPs were asked to give an overall assessment of the patient's quality of life in terms of whether the patient's quality of life had improved, worsened, or remained unchanged.

The results were stunning. The GPs' assessment was that all 75 patients had experienced an *improved* quality of life. The view from the close companions, however, was that 74 patients had a *worse* quality of life and *only one* patient had an improved quality of life. According to the patients, 36 believed that their quality of life had improved, seven reported that their quality of life had worsened, and 32 reported no change in their quality of life.

These results present a very sobering message to health professionals regarding the dangers of acting on their own assumptions in terms of the experiences of patients. The results also ring a cautionary bell regarding the extent to which the opinions of family and other close companions should be relied on for decision making with regard to health care services and the outcomes that are possible. In this study, GPs believed that the treatment they provided resulted in 100% of their patients having an improved quality of life, but only 48% of patients felt the same way. Also, 99% of the close companions believed that the patients' quality of life had deteriorated during the hypotensive therapy, but only 9% of patients felt the same way. Finally, none of the GPs or close companions thought that the patients' quality of life had remained unchanged, but almost half of the patients (43%) endorsed this response.

The treatment implications from this study in terms of appropriate and inappropriate care are clear. Making treatment decisions based on either the GPs' or the close companions' views of the patients' experiences would have led to inappropriate care in most cases. Regardless of the way in which the GP interprets a situation, it is the experience of the patient which is paramount. In this study, some patients reported that their quality of life had improved, and others reported that it had deteriorated (Jachuck et al., 1982). The only way to provide appropriate care in this instance is to listen to (and believe) the patient.

Thinking about communication in terms of listening and believing

Of course, listening to and believing the patient is an easy principle to accept but may be more difficult to apply in practice. There could be numerous reasons why a patient might provide a less than accurate report to her treating health professional about her experience of the treatment. In Chapter 2, the power imbalance that often exists between health professionals and patients was offered as one possible reason that patients might not always be as frank and forthright as they otherwise could be. Perhaps, also, a patient might not want to disappoint the health professional with whom she is working. Or it could be that a patient has had an experience of not being believed by her health professional in the past so she now reports what she anticipates the professional is expecting to hear. Maybe the patient is concerned that if she accurately reports her treatment experience then even more invasive procedures will be recommended.

For a variety of reasons, the importance of educating and informing the public about the centrality of their perspectives to their own health care cannot be too strongly emphasised. I mentioned this point in Chapter 2 and will refer to it again in Chapter 9 because it is an essential component of creating the change that is needed. In concert with this ongoing education, however, it is essential that health professionals honour their commitment to patient-perspective health care and follow the lead of the patient in determining the structure and nature of treatment.

There are also ways of listening to people such as patients that do not rely solely on the words these people provide when answering the questions they are asked. The manner in which they answer your questions can be important. Are they hesitant and awkward when replying for example? Do they look away or maintain eye contact in a relaxed, appropriate manner? Furthermore, they may volunteer information conversationally that provides an indication of the way in which they are currently experiencing their lives. Perhaps they mention going out more or joining a new club or finding greater satisfaction at work. Additionally, paying attention to aspects of their behaviour and appearance, particularly with regard to any changes that might occur over time, can sometimes provide useful information. Do they seem to be taking more or less interest in their appearance? Are they putting on or losing weight? Are they more or less active than they were before? These observations, combined with the answers they provide to your questions and the information they offer conversationally, can be used to develop a more complete understanding of the impact of the treatment they are receiving.

Recognising the dynamic nature of things we have regarded as static

Another reason that the patient's perspective is so crucial to understanding the appropriateness or otherwise of particular health care services with regard to quality of life is the way in which the quality of life construct is conceptualised. Allison, Locker, and Feine (1997) argue persuasively that quality of life is a dynamic rather than a static construct. This means that a person's frame of reference with regard to their quality of life can change over time so that what was considered a reasonable quality of life in one instance might, after certain experiences, be deemed to be a less than satisfactory quality of life or, indeed, a more than satisfactory quality of life. Sometimes the changes can be paradoxical and unexpected such as when patients with various illnesses report a higher quality of life than the quality of life reported by apparently healthy people. Furthermore, the factors that contribute to a person's quality of life can change. Allison et al. (1997) use the example of a person describing "family and social life, work, health, and financial circumstances" as the things that make the most important contributions to his quality of life but after being diagnosed and treated for laryngeal cancer, changing the important components to "being able to speak and eat, family and social life, and spiritual happiness". Recognising the fluidity of a concept such as quality of life provides further justification for the importance ascribed to the patient's perspective.

Cultural considerations

The primacy of the patient's perspective and the dangers inherent in ignoring it become even more obvious when cultural factors are considered. Ethan Watters' (2010) excellent book, *Crazy Like Us: The Globalization of the Western Mind*, provides an engaging and compelling account of the problems that occur when a Western concept of mental illness is imposed on other cultures. While the entire book communicates a powerful message, the chapter describing the infestation of the concept of post-traumatic stress disorder on the Sri Lankan psyche is especially moving. Watters (2010) points out that, because of the long period of civil unrest in Sri Lanka, Sri Lankans actually had sophisticated and nuanced ways of understanding and addressing trauma effectively. These indigenous approaches, however, were different from Western approaches. When the tsunami devastated Sri Lanka, large numbers of people wanting to provide support and assistance arrived in Sri Lanka from countries such as Australia, New Zealand, and the United States. Because Sri Lankans did not have the same language of trauma that the Western people had, the people from the West assumed that the Sri Lankans were ignorant of trauma, its impact, and how best to address it. Consequently, they set about "educating" the Sri Lankans about trauma and treating Sri Lankans considered traumatised by the tsunami with Western treatments. The results were astounding. While there may have been a great deal of good that came out of the presence of the Western visitors, there is also evidence of what can only be described as inappropriate care. Here is a particularly startling illustration from Watters (2010) book of what I am claiming to be inappropriate care:

> The juxtaposition of these well-meaning Western healers with the devastated landscape was sometimes breathtaking. Here, for instance is how Jennifer Baggerly, an assistant counselling professor at the University of Florida, recounted arriving in the remote village of Kalladi, where 215 families were living in a refugee camp. "'The suffering here was clear,' she writes. 'Rows of white canvas tents in the sweltering sun face a water tank that has been empty for a month and a half. Clean water access is a long walk away so children were thirsty and had unwashed clothes and hair. Some children had a chronic cough while others had sores on their bodies.' She then describes her team's psychological intervention, providing 'temporary relief from the suffering by conducting our puppet show, helping them make coping bracelets and magazine collages, playing active games, teaching them yoga, and passing out candy and toys to each child.'
>
> (Watters, 2010, p. 97)

It is hard to imagine that, with coughs, sores, and difficulty accessing clean water, the Sri Lankan families in this refugee camp would have considered puppet shows and coping bracelets to be appropriate care.

With Australian Aboriginal and Torres Strait Islander people, similar cultural differences exist with regard to mental health specifically and, indeed, the concept of health more generally. For Aboriginal and Torres Strait Islander Australians, the holistic concept of cultural, social, and emotional well-being (CSEWB) is preferred to the concept of mental health (Carey, 2013a). CSEWB includes seven domains relating to an individual's connection to important aspects of their lives (Gee, Dudgeon, Schultz, Hart, and Kelly, 2014). The domains are connection to body; connection to mind and emotions; connection to family and kinship; connection to community; connection to culture; connection to country; and connection to spirit, spirituality, and ancestors (Gee et al., 2014). Understanding psychological distress and addressing it effectively from the perspective of Aboriginal and Torres Strait Islander Australians necessitates an appreciation of these important domains.

It is significant to note that, traditionally, Aboriginal and Torres Strait Islander societies did not have a word or expression for the Western concept of health (Carey, 2013b). The National Health Strategy Working Party explain in their influential publication, *A National Aboriginal Health Strategy 1989*, that "health" to Aboriginal and Torres Strait Islander people concerns being able to determine all aspects of their lives. Moreover, quality of life is an important component of health to Aboriginal and Torres Strait Islander people (National Health Strategy Working Party, 1989).

It has been argued that self-determination, or control, is essential to health (Carey, 2016). Obviously, control of physiological variables such as body temperature, blood oxygen levels, and blood glucose levels is essential to health. What is less clearly recognised is that control of psychological and social variables is also essential to health. As will be described in the next chapter, there is a robust theoretical account of how control works that explains the importance of control to life itself.

It is paramount, therefore, when providing health care in cross-cultural contexts, that the perspective of the patient is the mould that shapes the design and delivery of health services. Failure to acknowledge that patients from different cultures will almost certainly have different understandings of health, illness, and disease will result in inappropriate care in many cases.

In 2010 at the Katherine Hospital in the Northern Territory, Australia, more than 25% of Aboriginal and Torres Strait Islander patients left the hospital before completing treatment (Cohen, 2017). Again, it should be noted here that whether or not treatment had been completed was determined by the service providers not the service recipients. One of the important factors in these "take own leave" situations was stated to be Aboriginal and Torres Strait Islander patients' perceptions of inadequate treatment (Cohen, 2017). In the Northern Territory generally, 11% of Aboriginal and Torres Strait Islander patients discharge themselves against medical advice, and, nationally, racism has been cited as a contributing factor in the low rates of Aboriginal and Torres Strait Islander people accessing health services (Cohen, 2017). Thankfully, there is a happy ending to the Katherine Hospital story. After an extensive investigation, specialist doctors who engaged with the community were employed, interpreters were used regularly, families were consulted regarding complex treatment plans, and the "take own leave" patients reduced to 4% (Cohen, 2017). Taking seriously the importance of the patient's perspective seemed to be an essential component of this remarkable and very encouraging turnaround.

There are stark reminders every day in clinical practice that patients do not always share the same understanding of health care services as their treating clinicians. As mentioned in

Chapter 1, when medications are prescribed, patient adoption of the medication protocol ranges from 0% to 100% with an average of 50% (Nieuwlaat et al., 2014). This means that a great deal of prescription medication is not being used as the treating clinician intended.

Understandings can differ with regard to the processes of health care contexts in addition to the content of what might be exchanged in these settings. Ardilo (2005), for examples, argues that cultural values underlie the interactions involved when assessing the cognitive functioning of individuals. The speed of processing which is considered ideal, for example, can vary across cultures (Ardilo, 2005). Also, in some cultures, creative answers are valued above obvious ones. Furthermore, the dynamic of asking someone a question to which the asker already knows the answer is not a common interaction across all cultures. Factors such as these can seriously compromise the accuracy of test results when conducted cross-culturally and can lead to erroneous conclusions being made about an individual's capabilities.

Missed appointments

Missed appointments are another costly indicator of a divergence in perspective between patients and treating health professionals. It has been estimated, for example, that approximately £600 million is lost each year in revenue for the National Health Service in the United Kingdom because of missed appointments (Gbolade, 2010). Missed appointments are especially problematic in mental health services where non-attendance of first appointments is reported to range from 16% to 67% (Hampton-Robb, Qualls, and Compton, 2003). Even when patients attend their first appointment, attendance at subsequent appointments is far from guaranteed. Ironically, even though the large-scale and expensive mental health service reform program in the United Kingdom is called "Improving Access to Psychological Therapies

(IAPT)," non-attendance rates of 47% have been reported (Richards and Borglin, 2011). The purported mechanism by which IAPT is supposed to improve access is through a stepped care approach to service delivery, yet in Richards' and Borglin's study, at every step, approximately 27% of patients did not turn up, did not come back, or dropped out (bearing in mind the difficulties with the term "treatment dropout" mentioned in Chapter 3). In this study, of the 7,859 people referred for services, only 4,183 (53%) received two or more sessions of assessment and then treatment (Richards and Borglin, 2011). To understand these results sensibly, it is essential to learn about the patients' perspectives. Marshall and his colleagues, for example, interviewed 14 patients from six different IAPT services (Marshall et al., 2015). The 14 patients interviewed had been referred to the respective IAPT service but had not attended at all or had attended only one appointment. Not being listened to was identified as a major barrier in the development of a good working relationship (Marshall et al., 2015). In Chapter 7, I will discuss appointment scheduling for psychological treatment in detail as one area that could benefit markedly from a patient–perspective redesign.

The balance between benefits and harms

For many treatments, there is a balance between benefits and harms. Brownlee et al. (2017) remind us that different patients will come to different conclusions regarding the way in which potential benefits and acceptable harms should be assessed. Furthermore, it appears to be the case that clinicians frequently lack an accurate appreciation of patients' values and preferences. Health professionals often make incorrect assumptions about whether or not patients would prefer to avoid aggressive or invasive interventions in some instances and whether they would choose more rather than less care in other cases (Brownlee et al., 2017). Brownlee et al. go so far as to call this "preference misdiagnosis" and report that it contributes to both the overuse and underuse of services.

Concluding comments

So, there are compelling reasons both clinically and empirically to adopt a patient-perspective approach to health care. There are also profound theoretical reasons that explain and justify the importance of this approach. Understanding the importance of an individual's perspective theoretically provides the inescapable conclusion that it is not the geographical positioning of patients but their perspectives that are essential to the provision of appropriate health care.

References

Allison, P. J., Locker, D., & Feine, J. S. (1997). Quality of life: A dynamic construct. *Social Science & Medicine*, *45*(2), 221–230.

Ardilo, A. (2005). Cultural values underlying psychometric cognitive testing. *Neuropsychology Review*, *15*(4), 185–195.

Brownlee, S., Chalkidou, K., Doust, J., Elshaug, A. G., Glasziou, P., Heath, I., ... Korenstein, D. (2017). Evidence for overuse of medical services around the world. *Lancet*, Published online 8 January. http://dx.doi.org/10.1016/S0140-6736(16)32585-5

Carey, T. A. (2013a). A qualitative study of a social and emotional wellbeing service for remote Indigenous Australians: Implications for access, effectiveness, and sustainability. *BMC Health Services Research*, *13*, 80. doi:10.1186/1472-6963-13-80. Retrieved from www.biomedcentral.com/1472-6963/13/80

Carey, T. A. (2013b). Defining Australian indigenous wellbeing: Do we *really* want the answers? Implications for policy and practice. *Psychotherapy and Politics International*, *11*(3), 182–194.

Carey, T. A. (2016). Health is control. *Annals of Behavioural Science*, *2*(1), 1–3.

Cohen, H. (2017). How Katherine Hospital, once Australia's worst for indigenous health, became one of the best. *Background Briefing*. ABC News. Retrieved May 5, 2017, from www.abc.net.au/news/2017-03-28/katherine-hospital-from-worst-in-the-country-to-one-of-the-best/8392792

Gbolade, B. A. (2010). A snap audit of "did not attend" patients in a gynecologic outpatient clinic. *Clinical Audit*, *2*, 93–96.

Gee, G., Dudgeon, P., Schultz, C., Hart, A., & Kelly, K. (2014). Aboriginal and Torres Strait Islander social and emotional wellbeing. In P. Dudgeon, H. Milroy, and R. Walker (Eds.), *Working together: Aboriginal and Torres Strait Islander mental health and wellbeing principles and practice* (2nd ed., pp. 55–68). Canberra: Commonwealth of Australia.

Hampton-Robb, S., Qualls, R. C., & Compton, W. C. (2003). Predicting first-session attendance: The influence of referral source and client income. *Psychotherapy Research*, *13*, 223–233.

Jachuck, S. J., Brierley, H., Jachuck, S., & Willcox, P. M. (1982). The effect of hypotensive drugs on the quality of life. *Journal of the Royal College of General Practitioners*, *32*, 103–105.

Marshall, D., Quinn, C., Child, S., Shenton, D., Pooler, J., Forber, S., & Byng, R. (2015). What IAPT services can learn from those who do not attend. *Journal of Mental Health*, *25*(5), 410–415.

National Health Strategy Working Party. (1989). *A national Aboriginal health strategy 1989*. Canberra, Australia: Office of Aboriginal and Torres Strait Islander Health.

Nieuwlaat, R., Wilczynski, N., Navarro, T., Hobson, N., Jeffery, R., Keepanasseril, A., ... Haynes, R. B. (2014). Interventions for enhancing medication adherence. *Cochrane Database of Systematic Reviews*, Issue 11 (Art. No.: CD000011). doi:10.1002/14651858.CD000011.pub4

Richards, D. A., & Borglin, G. (2011). Implementation of psychological therapies for anxiety and depression in routine practice: Two year prospective cohort study. *Journal of Affective Disorders*, *133*(1–2), 51–60.

Watters, E. (2010). *Crazy like us: The globalization of the Western mind*. New York: Free Press.

5

THE THEORETICAL UNDERPINNINGS OF PATIENT-PERSPECTIVE CARE

To know the best way to treat something, it is important to accurately understand how that something functions. I once learned first-hand how problematic it can be, for example, to put diesel fuel in a car that is designed to use petrol. When something, such as a car, a washing machine, or a television, is functioning well, then appreciating the intricacies of how it works is not so important. When performance falters, however, your ability to correct the malfunction will depend directly on how precisely you grasp the essentials of its operations. I have almost no appreciation of how a car engine works, so I make sure I regularly take my car to a facility that has people who do have the required skills and expertise. I don't take my car to an orthodontist, a sous-chef de cuisine, or a cabinetmaker even though these people might have exceptional talents in particular areas. Rather, I take my car to a mechanic who has the knowledge and acumen to detect and correct any mechanical problems that might exist.

The extent to which our health system is faltering in terms of the costly, harmful, and widespread delivery of inappropriate care is strong evidence that our current understanding of how humans function, and how that functioning can be disrupted, is crucially inadequate. If we are going to make the necessary changes in a way that is sustainable, then different technology is required. We're in a similar situation to the pickle someone might be in if they were trying to repair a convection microwave oven with the manual for a front-loading washing machine. To borrow a concept from a popular piece of children's literature, we're "in the wrong book"!

The importance of values and preferences

I have suggested in this book, a sentiment that is echoed in other sources: that patients' values and preferences are a critical component of the design, development, and delivery of appropriate care. Why should this be the case? Given the amount of training health professionals undertake, why should they not be able to adroitly determine the most effective and efficient health service for a particular patient in any given context? Moreover, why are concepts such as self-determination and empowerment considered to be so important with regard to health service delivery? My car mechanic spends no time at all attempting to understand the intentions of my Toyota Prado when I book it in for a service. Nor has he ever discussed with me any empowerment strategies I should adopt with the Prado. If, as has been proposed, health care is ultimately about helping people maintain states that are necessary to achieve the goals that are important to them, then the reason that preferences and values are so important must have something to do with goals. Mechanics don't need to bother themselves with what the goals of motor vehicles might be because motor vehicles don't have goals. The drivers of motor vehicles have goals, and motor vehicles can be used to achieve goals, but a motor vehicle itself is devoid of goals. This line of reasoning would suggest that an essential aspect of correcting the situation regarding the provision of inappropriate health care will necessarily involve knowledge about what a goal is and the effect it has within the system of a behaving entity.

A theory of human functioning that is intimately connected with goal specification and realisation is Perceptual Control Theory (PCT; Powers, 2005). PCT describes "control" as a phenomenon of the natural world. Indeed, organic, autonomous control is the natural phenomenon that separates living from non-living things (Carey, Mansell, and Tai, 2015). Anything that lives, from a humble single cell to a majestic blue whale, to keep on living, must be able to control the state of its internal environment while situated within an unpredictably changing external environment.

Why this particular theory?

So why pluck this particular theory out of obscurity to support something as momentous as a paradigm shift in health care? There are very strong reasons for basing ideas about the reform of health care on PCT. A more complete justification will develop as you read through the rest of the chapter, but for now, it is important to understand that control is mentioned ubiquitously throughout health care, yet there are almost no theoretical explanations about how control works. Marmot (2006), for example, describes control and social engagement as an organising principle for the social determinants of health but provides only empirical, rather than theoretical, support for this. Empirical evidence is certainly important, but an initiative that is based on *both* empirical and theoretical evidence is in a much stronger position than one based only on empirical or theoretical support.

PCT has a very strong evidence base and, in a fashion of unparalleled rigour in the life sciences, PCT principles have been tested through the exacting methods of simulation model building (e.g., Marken, 2014; Powers, 1998). Rather than building conceptual or statistical models, PCT scientists build *functional* models – models that actually work. In PCT, instead of the descriptive models that are standard fare in the life sciences, a model is considered to be "a precise quantitative proposal about the way some system operates in relation to its environment" (Bourbon and Powers, 1993, p. 51). In this sense, PCT models are *generative* because "the proposed organization is stated in a way that can be used to calculate behaviour as a function of moment-by-moment variations in the independent variable. By that usage, a model does not substitute for knowledge. To the contrary, simulation of a well-posed model rigorously tests one's presumed knowledge of the causal principles at work in behaviour" (Bourbon and Powers, 1993, p. 51). For reasons, therefore, of unrivalled rigour and explanatory power, PCT principles are the essential backbone of the patient-perspective paradigm.

How control works

PCT is the theoretical explanation of how control actually works in the natural world. The basic building block of control is the closed causal negative feedback loop (Carey, 2008; Carey et al., 2015; Powers, 2005). The configuration of this unit is known as a control system. Powers' (2005) insightful, revolutionary, and confronting discovery was that organic control systems control their input, *not* their output. PCT, then, is an explanation of behaviour from a first-person perspective. Unlike other theories and models that offer a third-person, or observer's perspective, of behaviour, PCT is a tale of biological functioning from the inside looking out rather than the outside looking on. So, PCT is, ultimately, an account of the *effect* or the *consequences* of the behaviour *for the behaving entity* rather than a statement about the behaviour itself. Or, more precisely, PCT is an explanation of how it is that a living thing can produce reliable results in an unreliable environment.

A detailed exploration of PCT is outside the remit of this book; however, excellent resources are available for people who want to know more about the theory. Some high-quality websites are www.iapct.org, www.pctweb.org, and www.mindreadings.com. A website outlining a psychological treatment based on the principles of PCT is www.methodoflevels.com.au. Some of the information on these websites includes journal articles and books that provide numerous explanations of the theory in varying levels of detail. There is also a blog on the Psychology Today website called *In Control* (www.psychologytoday.com/blog/in-control) that provides short, easy-to-read articles on different aspects and applications of the theory. The purpose of the current chapter is to outline the basic principles of the theory and describe their relevance and importance to the provision of appropriate health care.

PCT suggests that three fundamental processes occur simultaneously and interdependently in a configuration of circular, rather than linear, causality for control to arise. The processes are perception, comparison, and action (Powers, 1998). Control systems control things that vary, and things that vary are called variables. It's often difficult to appreciate just how variable our habitats are, or could be, because we are so good at controlling them (and preventing or minimising the variability that would otherwise occur). As a thought experiment, think about what your appearance would like if you did nothing at all to affect it from now until this time next week. Or think about what the state of your dwelling would look like if you took no action at all to alter the way it appeared for an entire seven days: no picking things up, no dusting, no wiping benches, no putting things away. Or imagine how your car might behave as you travel at speed down the motorway if you suddenly decided to stop exerting some influence on how fast and in what direction it moved. Environments don't vary anywhere nearly as much as they could because of the skilful controlling of the controllers who are resident in these environments.

For some variable state of the environment to be controlled, the variable must be *perceived*, the current state of the variable must be *compared* with a desired state (or goal), and the controlling entity must be able to *act* to affect the perceived state so that it matches the desired state. Life is a never-ending process of minimising the difference between what is perceived and what is specified. Another way of expressing this is to say that all our actions are involved in keeping the difference between what we want and what we've got (at every point in time) very small. Or we act to make the way things *are* (as we perceive them to be) be the way they *should be*. A driver keeps her car on the road by *perceiving* where the car is on the road (driving with one's eyes closed is never very successful for very long), *comparing* the current position of the car with the desired position of the car, and *acting* so that the perception of where the car is matches the specification of where the car should be.

In a very real sense, life is one ongoing, complex, and multifactorial Goldilocks' story. Goldilocks was the little girl who discovered some porridge in the bears' house and found that one bowl of porridge was *too hot*, one bowl of porridge was *too cold*, and one bowl of porridge was *just right*. We all have our own *just right* states about all of the things that we control. We have just right states for our relationships, our physical appearance, our diet, our activity level, our emotions, our blood glucose level, and so on. Health professionals have just right states for the type of health professional they want to be. This means, on an ongoing basis, health professionals are perceiving the health professional they are being *right now*, comparing that with the health professional they want to be, and acting to keep *being* and *want to be* the same. Some GPs, for example, might prescribe antibiotics for viral infections not because they think the antibiotics will be effective but because they want to perceive themselves as being helpful in the company of an insistent patient. Understanding interactions in a health care environment from a control perspective provides crucial clues as to how these environments could be improved.

One of the important but neglected features of health care is that service provision almost exclusively occurs within the context of a *relationship*. PCT has an important contribution to make to the way we understand relationships. Essentially, a relationship involves at least two people controlling their own perceptions by controlling other people (Marken and Carey, 2015). Understanding relationships from a control perspective provides a very helpful and constructive way of understanding interactions such as cooperation and conflict and provokes an optimistic attitude to phenomena such as disengagement and resistance (Marken and Carey, 2015).

Important features of the phenomenon of control

Controlling variables need not be a completely conscious activity either. Important parts of our system are able to perceive, compare, and act with regard to the speed and position of our car, for example, while we occupy our minds with things like the busy daily schedule ahead of us or the difficult conversation we just had. Furthermore, as I mentioned earlier, every living thing controls. Simple organisms control simple variables, while more sophisticated creatures are able to control abstract ideas such as love, compromise, compassion, and retribution. We're not aware of all of the different aspects of our functioning. We only "know" what we perceive. Quite literally, *life is all perception* (Powers, 1998).

To survive and flourish, a living thing must *vary* its output so that its input does not vary or varies systematically. In practical terms, this means that we do *not* control our behaviour. We *vary* our behaviour so that what we are sensing or experiencing *is* controlled. Returning to the simple example of driving a car will help illustrate this fundamental principle. When people drive, they control certain variable aspects of their driving experience such as the speed of their car, how far behind the car in front they are, and the position of their car relative to the side of the road. To control each of these things, they undoubtedly *use* their actions, but it is impossible to specify ahead of time what the angle of their foot on the accelerator pedal will be or how and when they will turn the steering wheel. To drive successfully, people must be prepared to vary the way they are acting according to the situations they encounter in the environment as they drive along. Suppose you were somehow able to program into your muscles the precise actions that successfully moved your car from home to work on Monday. If you then reprogrammed your muscles on Tuesday (or Wednesday or Thursday or even the next Monday) to produce exactly the same muscle forces that were produced on Monday, your car probably wouldn't make it to the end of your street before a mishap occurred.

We are so good at making things happen the way we want that we rarely notice that that is what we are doing. Actually, every living entity is good at making things happen the way it wants, or it doesn't continue living. It seems a little odd to describe a single cell as "wanting" something, yet a single cell has specifications for the state in which its internal environment must be maintained if it is to continue existing. Even a single cell is able to vary what it sends out to its environment so that what the environment sends back to it does not disturb its internal state.

Examples of control in nature

Here's a particularly evocative description of control provided by Powers (1992). It's an example from Powers demonstrated to him by the martins and hummingbirds that used to frequent his backyard.

> I used to have a martin house (blue martins, not taylor martins) in my back yard. Those birds often wouldn't bother to use the perch: they'd fly up to the hole, fold their wings, and pop in without touching the sides. Consider the precision of control that's needed to do that from an infinitely variable set of starting positions and trajectories. How accurately do you think the aerodynamic forces of the wings had to be adjusted to make a twenty foot approach curve on a breezy day go within a quarter of an inch of the center of the hole? I never saw a bird miss a try.
>
> Or look at a hummingbird. It is frozen in the air near the flower. When it's feeding, its head and beak are nailed to the flower in absolute immobility, while the body moves slightly around, and the wings continue their blur of action. How precisely do you think the forces from the beating wings and the little body movements cancel disturbances from the wind? It's hard to see any movement of the head at all; the bird can detect and correct smaller errors than you can see. And then the bird suddenly backs off six inches to a new frozen position, swoops twenty feet and runs into another invisible stone wall, and so on as long as you care to watch it.
>
> (Powers, 1992, p. 257)

Control and health

To fully appreciate the phenomenon of control and understand how far-reaching its implications are, it may be useful to define the phenomenon. Powers' (2005) formal definition of control is: achievement and maintenance of a preselected perceptual state in the controlling system, through actions on the environment that also cancel the effects of disturbances (p. 296). Colloquially, an equivalent definition might be something like "making things happen the way you want" (Carey et al., 2015).

A link between control and health was introduced in the previous chapter. Now, with definitions of control in mind, the relevance of control to health is revealed. At every level of life, ". . . control is health. Health is control" (Carey, 2016, p. 2). A healthy cell is one that is able to achieve and maintain essential internal states. A healthy body achieves and maintains particular conditions such as body temperature and blood oxygen levels. A healthy person is able to achieve and maintain psychological and social states associated with optimism, contentment, motivation, cooperation, and so on. Given the ubiquity of negative feedback control in nature, it has been identified as a genuine, functional bio–psycho–social model that has important implications for individual and social functioning (Carey, Mansell, and Tai, 2014).

A recap

At this point, the problems of inappropriate health care have been outlined, and a rigorous theoretical rationale for patient-perspective care has been provided. Given the foundations that have been laid, the implications that this particular theoretical approach has to health systems and services can now be described. The following chapter provides a comprehensive, but perhaps not exhaustive, list of the way in which a patient-perspective approach, informed by the principles of PCT, could reconfigure the design and delivery of health services to ensure the routine provision of appropriate health care.

References

Bourbon, W. T., & Powers, W. T. (1993). Models and their worlds. *Closed Loop*, *3*(1), 45–72. Retrieved May 30, 2017, from www.pctresources.com/Journals/Files/Closed_Loop/Closed_Loop_print/Closed_Loop_vol3_%231_print.pdf

Carey, T. A. (2008). *Hold that thought! Two steps to effective counseling and psychotherapy with the method of levels*. Chapel Hill, NC: Newview Publications.

Carey, T. A. (2016). Health is control. *Annals of Behavioural Science, 2*(1), 1–3.

Carey, T. A., Mansell, W., & Tai, S. J. (2014). A biopsychosocial model based on negative feedback and control. *Frontiers of Human Neuroscience, 8*, article 94. doi:10.3389/fnhum.2014.00094 http://journal.frontiersin.org/Journal/10.3389/fnhum.2014.00094/abstract

Carey, T. A., Mansell, W., & Tai, S. J. (2015). *Principles-based counselling and psychotherapy: A method of levels approach.* London: Routledge.

Marken, R. S. (2014). *Doing research on purpose: A control theory approach to experimental psychology.* St Louis, MO: New View.

Marken, R. S., & Carey, T. A. (2015). *Controlling people: The paradoxical nature of being human.* Brisbane: Australian Academic Press.

Marmot, M. (2006). Health in an unequal world: Social circumstances, biology and disease. *Clinical Medicine, 6*(6), 559–572.

Powers, W. T. (1992, 26 March). *CSGnet archives.* Retrieved June 2, 2017, from www.pctresources.com/CSGnet/Files/CSGnet_archive/CSGnet_pdf_files/CSG_9203.pdf

Powers, W. T. (1998). *Making sense of behaviour: The meaning of control.* New Canaan, CT: Benchmark.

Powers, W. T. (2005). *Behavior: The control of perception* (2nd ed.). New Canaan, CT: Benchmark.

6

WHAT PATIENT-PERSPECTIVE CARE MEANS IN PRACTICE

PCT's relevance, both directly and indirectly, to appropriate health care service provision, is far reaching. PCT overturns some well-known and long-standing attitudes and beliefs. Concepts such as the Golden Rule, empathy, and objectivity are all significantly revised when viewed through a PCT lens. While these three ideas do not pertain specifically or only to health care, they have a significant impact on the relationship between patients and health care professionals, which is one of the main factors that needs to change if the amount of inappropriate health care is to be reduced in a meaningful and lasting way. Other attitudes and beliefs regarding service provision in health care will be altered within a PCT-informed, patient-perspective health care paradigm. Table 6.1 provides a list of some of the important ways in which the patient-perspective approach differs from the current patient-centred mind-set. There is overlap, sometimes substantially so, between some of the patient-perspective characteristics in Table 6.1. Given that this volume is an introduction to the area, for the purpose of clarity, I considered it would be most helpful to discuss each of these areas separately even if, as the work in this field progresses, some of these attributes are combined.

Each of the characteristics in Table 6.1 will be explained in detail throughout this chapter. It is perhaps more accurate to think of each of the rows in Table 6.1 as demarcating the

Table 6.1 Differences between the patient-centred and patient-perspective approaches to health care.

Patient-Centred Approach	Patient-Perspective Approach
Golden Rule: "Do unto others as you would have done unto you"	Golden Rule: "Do unto others as they would have done unto themselves"
Empathy	Considered curiosity
Objective	Inter-subjective
Self-determination is a basic human right	Self-determination is a fundamental property of the way in which we are designed
Third-person perspective	First-person perspective
Health professional teaches, coaches, and guides	Health professional learns
Patient is at the centre of decisions about treatment design and delivery	Patient perspective determines treatment design and delivery
Patients are engaged	Patients are invited
Mistakes should be avoided; risk should be prioritised, managed, and prevented	Mistakes and risk are inevitable features of life

Patient-Centred Approach	*Patient-Perspective Approach*
Patients are empowered	Patients are acknowledged to be controllers
Health professionals' standards of health inform treatment	Individual patients' standards of health inform treatment
Health services are applied to patients	Health services are available to patients

endpoints of various continua rather than representing a number of distinct dichotomies. Some, such as the Golden Rule, could be considered to be dichotomous, but others, such as teaching and coaching rather than learning, are perhaps more continuous. Regardless of the way in which each of these qualities is conceptualised, however, it is my stance throughout this book that the more health professionals within a particular health service or system emulate the qualities in the patient-perspective column rather than the patient-centred column, the more effective, efficient, and appropriate health care provision will be. Table 6.1 could even function as a guide to reflective self-assessment whereby health professionals assess the extent to which they practice from a patient-perspective paradigm or whether their practices indicate a patient-centred approach. Table 6.2 provides a summary of the details that are provided in the following paragraphs and explicitly highlights some of the important implications for the practice of adopting a patient-perspective approach to service provision.

The Golden Rule

Various forms of the Golden Rule exist in many different religions and philosophies. The general spirit of the Golden Rule

is "Do unto others as you would have done unto you" or, colloquially, "Treat others the way you want to be treated". Health
professionals subscribing to this ideal could feel justified in making decisions about their patients based on what they think they
would do if they were in a similar situation. So, oncologists might
think about the treatment they would prefer if they receive a
diagnosis of terminal cancer.

Given how far we have now come in this book and the mate-
rial we have covered, you might be able to recognise for yourself
the flaw in the conventional framing of the Golden Rule. The
fact is, we are *not* all the same, and it is a mistake to assume that
we have uniform goals. What I want in a particular situation *may*
be similar to what you want, but it is also likely to be different

Table 6.2 Patient-perspective health care characteristics and their implications
for practice.

Patient-Perspective Characteristics	Implications for Practice
Golden Rule: "Do unto others as they would have done unto themselves"	Health professionals monitor, in an ongoing manner, the extent to which they treat patients the way the patients want to be treated. Tests are conducted and treatments delivered based on the patients', not the professionals', preferences.
Considered curiosity	Empathy is not considered relevant or possible. Health professionals value and adopt a stance of considered curiosity in their interactions with patients.
Inter-subjective	Health professionals understand that they do not have a privileged "objective" perspective when it comes to considering health care decisions. They seek, in an ongoing manner, to increase their awareness of both their own subjective perspective as well as the patient's subjective perspective.

Patient-Perspective Characteristics	Implications for Practice
Self-determination is a fundamental feature of the way in which we are designed	Health professionals strive to understand the preferences, priorities, and values being served by patients' self-determining activity and seek to remove any barriers that might otherwise compromise this activity.
First-person perspective	Health professionals understand that the meaning of behaviour can only be obtained by considering the perspective of the behaver rather than the perspective of an observer.
Health professional learns	Health professionals understand that they are not the arbiters of what is best for patients. They minimise the extent to which they teach, coach, and guide and maximise the time they spend enquiring, offering, and following.
Patient perspective determines treatment design and delivery	Health professionals provide services based on the priorities and preferences of the patients.
Patients are invited	Health professionals persistently and warmly invite patients to make use of the health care resources when they need to.
Mistakes and risk are inevitable features of life	Health professionals understand that patients won't always act the way the health professional thinks they should. Health professionals manage risks according to their professional and organisational standards based on the patient's first-person perspective of the mistake or risk.
Patients are acknowledged to be controllers	Health professionals endorse the inherent controlling nature of both themselves and their patients and minimise the extent to which they thwart or impede these controlling tendencies.

(Continued)

Table 6.2 (Continued)

Patient-Perspective Characteristics	Implications for Practice
Individual patients' standards of health inform treatment	Health professionals use the standards of individual patients rather than arbitrary population-based norms to guide decisions about appropriate protocols and procedures.
Health services are available to patients	Health professionals promote the availability of health services to patients to enable patients to achieve the goals they seek to experience.

in important ways. The PCT version of the Golden Rule would be "Do unto others *as they would have done unto themselves*" or "Treat others the way they *want to be treated*". This version of the Golden Rule, of course, implies that health professionals would need to spend time finding out how patients want to be treated and providing them with the necessary information to make an informed decision. This is entirely the point. Health care delivered from a PCT perspective would involve a great deal of time finding out how patients understand what it is they are experiencing and learning about the goals that effective, efficient, and appropriate health care could help them achieve.

Empathy

The concept of empathy permits a similar attitude to the Golden Rule, which is that of presuming to know or understand what another person is experiencing. The definition of "empathy" from dictionary.com that is relevant to this discussion is "the psychological identification with or vicarious experiencing of the feelings, thoughts, or attitudes of another". Again, from a PCT perspective, we would assume we can *never* experience, vicariously or otherwise, the feelings, thoughts, and attitudes of

another. Ironically, the more empathic we are as health professionals, the more likely we are to assume we know, or understand,
what our patients are going through – and consequently, the *less*
likely we will be to enquire with genuine, considered curiosity.
Curiosity is genuine if it is motivated only by a desire to learn or
know, and it is considered if it is focussed and responsive to the
needs and interests of the other person. Curiosity needs to be
focussed because, in a health setting, not all information is relevant, and it needs to be responsive because some individuals may
give indications, for example, that they do not want their health
professionals to learn or know more about them. The role of a
health professional in our current system, however, is very much
to assume they can know what their patients are going through
and then, based on that knowledge, instruct and advise their
patients rather than listening and learning from their patients.

Objectivity

The idea of an objective stance or perspective is another ubiq-
uitous theme in the health industry. Often it seems to be used
in the sense of the health professional having an "objective"
view of the patient's problem with the implication being that
this objective point of view is somehow superior and more
reliable and trustworthy than the patient's subjective opinion.
While there are a number of different ways in which the term
"objective" can be used, Velmans (2009) makes the point that
science can never be objective in the sense of being "observer
free". "Objective" can sometimes also be used to mean "dispassionate" or "impartial", but it is unlikely that there could
even be objectivity in the sense of a dispassionate or impartial attitude in a health care context. Even when a so-called
objective number such as 8.2, representing a patient's current
cholesterol level, is being discussed between a patient and a
general practitioner (GP), the number is very likely to have

different *meanings* between the GP and the patient. And even if the number means similar things to the GP and the patient, the fact that it has meaning at all disqualifies it from being "objective". The quality of life study by Jachuck and colleagues (1982) mentioned in Chapter 4 provides a sobering illustration of the dangers of ascribing primacy to the opinions of others. Velmans (2009) promotes the idea of *intersubjectivity* as a way of conceptualising shared activities that are always subjectively experienced.

As mentioned in Chapter 1, the PCT angle is that we are living subjectively in an objective world. That is, we can accept that there is a world "out there" beyond our senses that will still be there whether we are sensing it or not. We only ever know that world, however, through our senses. We can never experience the world directly. Living, in the final analysis, is subjective. So is "experience". The very act of experiencing something, anything, is subjective in that your experience of whatever it is you are experiencing is completely unique. "You are the only one on earth who experiences all of what is happening (by way of sensation) when you move your own personal forefinger" (Robertson and Powers, 1990, p. 31). Even if you and I are sitting side by side in the same cinema watching the same movie, it will be a different experience for both of us. For a start, I am in your environment, and you are in mine. Then the movie will mean different things, and resonate or clash, with the unique life experiences we have both had up until this point. We can never know for certainty what it is that another experiences, but we can commit to constantly working to understand more clearly the priorities and preferences of other people and how we might be able to help them achieve that which is important to them. We can never actually walk a mile, or any other distance, in another person's shoes. We can, however, walk beside them if they want us to, and we can pay attention to the path upon which they are guiding us.

Self-determination

The importance of self-determination is widely recognised. There is perhaps less attention devoted to *why* self-determination is important, but the fact that it *is* important is undisputed. The first thing to realise about self-determination, however, particularly with regard to the way we currently conceptualise health care, is that it is not *absolute* self-determination. This is self-determination within limits. In the document *A National Framework for Recovery-Oriented Mental Health Services: Guide for Practitioners and Providers* (Australian Health Ministers' Advisory Council (AHMAC), 2013), for example, self-determination is recognised as a "vital part of successful treatment", but "the principles of recovery emphasise choice and self-determination within medical–legal requirements and duty of care" (p. 3).

This conditional feature of self-determination creates a tension in health care that is difficult to reconcile. In the glossary of the national framework, for example, the definition of self-determination begins with "The right of individuals to have full power over their own lives". (AHMAC, 2013, p. 81). This definition, however, contradicts the earlier statement that situates self-determination within the context of medical–legal requirements and duty of care. If self-determination exists within medical–legal requirements and duty of care considerations, then, clearly, individuals do not have *full* power over their lives. At least, they only have that power as long as they are making decisions that do not disrupt the medical–legal and duty of care responsibilities of the health professional with whom they are working. This tension is acknowledged in the national framework document with an explicit statement that "A recovery orientation requires services to confront the tension between maximising choice and supporting positive risk-taking . . ." (AHMAC, 2013, p. 20). Even this acknowledgement, however, underscores the importance of a patient-perspective approach. For example, how is "positive risk-taking" to be judged? Positive from whose perspective? Surely, the positivity or otherwise of the risk-taking must be assessed in relation to an individual's goals and the life he is creating for himself.

It is legitimate to ask if we can ever have *absolute* self-determination. Surely, a responsible society is one in which people are encouraged to create the self-determined lives they desire in a way that does not prevent other people from doing the same thing. However, if a line needs to be drawn between the self-determining practices of an individual and the collective social good, where is the line to be drawn and who is to draw that line? Perhaps the first step in successfully negotiating this quandary is to recognise that the quandary exists. PCT will not provide prescriptive answers to this dilemma but it will help us consider the consequences of any line we decide to lay down.

A very slippery slope in health care service provision arises from the juxtaposition of the rights of an individual to self-determination and the medical-legal and duty of care responsibilities of a health professional. For example, Table 6.3 provides statements about self-determination and the right to withdraw from treatment that have been extracted from the ethical codes of professional psychology bodies in America, Canada, Britain, and Australia. Each code has a statement recognising the importance of self-determination, and all codes except the American code have an explicit statement about an individual's ability to withdraw from services. The ability to withdraw from services is endorsed more broadly than simply in psychology. The *National Practice Standards for the Mental Health Workforce, 2013* (Victorian Government Department of Health, 2013), for example, instructs mental health practitioners to advise people "of their right to refuse treatment" (p. 17).

Positioning self-determination within the boundaries of medical-legal and duty of care responsibilities means that, in practice, the ability to exercise one's right to refuse treatment is left to the discretion of the treating health professional. If, in the health professional's opinion, there are significant duty of care implications if the patient elects to withdraw from treatment, then the health professional is granted the authority to prevent an individual from exercising her right to withdraw thereby interfering with the patient's self-determining propensities. Syme (2004) was alert to this nuance when he discussed what he calls "control of destiny". By "control of destiny", Syme (2004) was referring to "the ability of people to deal with the forces that affect their lives, even if they decide not to deal with them" (p. 3).

Self-determination is not a property that comes into play only when patients are making the decisions that a health professional thinks they *should* make. We are *always* self-determining. Self-determination can certainly be compromised or diminished, but it is not like a light that can be switched on when it is needed and off when it is inconvenient or otherwise unwanted. Even when we find other people's behaviour objectionable, they are still self-determining.

The alternative to *self*-determining is interesting to contemplate. Would that be *other*-determining? Surely, the current situation in health services and systems with the widespread provision of inappropriate care has eventuated precisely because there is far too much other-determining occurring with regard to the tests and treatments that are delivered.

Self-determination is described as a "right" by three of the four ethical codes in Table 6.3. From a PCT perspective, however, self-determination is much more than a right. Given that, according to PCT, we are designed as living control systems, self-determination is a fundamental, inherent property of our design. Describing self-determination as a "right" is akin to suggesting that motor neurons have the right to transmit signals to muscle fibres, enzymes have the right to accelerate biochemical reactions, and kidneys have the right to regulate electrolytes in the blood.

We are designed to be self-determining. Thus, both patients *and* health professionals are self-determining creatures. And what we determine are the experiences that produce our expectations and preferences regarding the lives we'd like to be living. From

Table 6.3 Statements of self-determination and rights to refuse treatment in ethical codes of different psychological societies and associations.

Psychological Organisation	Self-Determination	Right to Refuse Treatment
American Psychological Association (2017)	"Psychologists respect the dignity and worth of all people, and the rights of individuals to privacy, confidentiality, and self-determination" (p. 4).	No clear statement made although informed consent is discussed and, with regard to treatment for which generally recognised techniques and procedures have not been established, psychologists should inform clients/patients of "the voluntary nature of their participation" (p. 14).
Australian Psychological Society (2007)	"Psychologists regard people as intrinsically valuable and respect their rights, including the right to autonomy and justice" (p. 11).	"*Psychologists* ensure consent is informed by: . . . (e) advising clients that they may participate, may decline to participate, or may withdraw from methods or procedures proposed to them" (p. 13).
British Psychological Society (2009)	"*Psychologists should:* . . . (i) Endeavour to support the self-determination of clients, while at the same time remaining alert to potential limits placed upon self-determination by personal characteristics or by externally imposed circumstances" (p. 14).	"*Psychologists should:* . . . (ii) Ensure from the first contact that clients are aware of their right to withdraw at any time from the receipt of professional services or from research participation" (p. 14).

Psychological Organisation	Self-Determination	Right to Refuse Treatment
Canadian Psychological Association (2000)	"Rights to privacy, self-determination, personal liberty, and natural justice are of particular importance to psychologists, and they have a responsibility to protect and promote these rights in all of their activities" (p. 8).	"Ensure, in the process of obtaining informed consent, that at least the following points are understood: . . . the option to refuse or withdraw at any time, without prejudice" (p. 11).

this point of view, all of our behaviour is part of an ongoing process of self-determination. Even brand-new babies have expectations about how much and how often they'd like to be fed, how much they'd like to be held, and so on. Despite their limited behavioural repertoire, they do whatever they can to experience the feeding and snuggling they crave.

Inevitably, difficulties arise when an entity is prevented from functioning as it is designed. Problems occur when a person's self-determining proclivities are restricted or otherwise interfered with just as surely as the complications that eventuate when a pancreas is prevented from producing insulin. Patient-perspective health care, therefore, seeks to ensure that the procedures and protocols that are offered to patients, enhance rather than inhibit patients' self-determining tendencies. Of course, if health care services are to have an enhancing rather than inhibiting effect, then health professionals will be required to gain an understanding of the preferences, priorities, and values being created and maintained through each patient's self-determining activity along with a commitment to honour the self-determining process of which they now play a part.

Whose perspective?

Many theories and models of behaviour adopt a third-person perspective of that which they endeavour to explain. This is an observer's perspective or an account of behaviour from the outside looking on. Even when goals and other motives are included in theoretical explanations, the ultimate object of explanation is still the behaviour that can be observed. PCT, however, is an explanation of the activity of living from a first-person perspective. That is, PCT describes how behaviour arises from the vantage point of the behaving entity. PCT depicts behaviour from the inside looking out rather than from the outside looking on.

It turns out that the perspective from which behaviour is considered is critical. To make sense of the behaviour that can be observed, it is essential to understand the effects that the behaviour is producing for the behaver. When someone misses a scheduled appointment, for example, is she disregarding the advice of their health professional, withdrawing from treatment, attending to an urgent and unexpected family obligation, engrossed in a favourite hobby, appeasing her employer's displeasure at her ongoing absence, balancing her budget, adjusting her priorities, protecting a relationship, or something else entirely? To have any impact on changing the number of missed appointments in a service, it is essential to obtain some appreciation of appointment missing from the patients' perspectives. Similarly, Griffith, Hutchinson, and Hastings (2013) argue that to understand challenging behaviour in ways that could inform policy and clinical practice, an "insider perspective" should be adopted.

Again, the study by Jachuck et al. (1982) provides a powerful illustration of why paying attention to the patient's first-person perspective is paramount to defining and delivering appropriate care. The only way to be clear about what someone is doing when we observe him behaving in particular ways is to appreciate the goal or expectation that is being tended. To understand patients more accurately, therefore, a health professional emulating a patient-perspective approach would persistently strive to grasp the patient's perspective. The objective here, for the health professional, is to consider the patient's behaviour on the patient's terms rather than assuming his own perspective of the patient's behaviour is authoritative.

Teaching, coaching, and guiding or learning

The roles and responsibilities of health professionals differ between the patient-centred and patient-perspective approaches. As mentioned earlier, however, the distinction here is perhaps more about when one places oneself along a continuum or the weightings one applies to different roles in different situations, rather than a dichotomous position involving a this-or-that decision. It is likely that to provide efficient, effective, and appropriate health care, at various times, a health professional may need to teach or coach or guide. Health professionals have knowledge and expertise that can undoubtedly be used by patients to help patients live the lives they seek. Within a patient-perspective paradigm, however, a health professional would, primarily, see her role as a learner. Before using their knowledge and expertise to provide any teaching, coaching, or guiding, she would need to learn a great deal about the patient and the life that the patient's health concerns are disrupting.

To reiterate what has been expressed previously, we can never know how it is to be another person. We can, however, seek to learn about the people who engage our services. We can listen to them describing their hopes and dreams and frustrations and achievements and troubles and disappointments, and we can offer our skills and services for them to use as they need to in order to achieve the things that are important to them.

Primarily, a patient-perspective health professional is considered to be a resource who patients can use to obtain desired outcomes. Health professionals often have important information that can be very helpful to patients. To know what information to provide, however, the health professional must understand what the patient wants. And to know whether or not the information is helping, it is imperative to have some grasp of how the information has been received and understood by the patient. In patient-centred health care, service providers frequently guide and lead based on an assumption that they know what will be best for patients. In patient-perspective health care, service providers enquire, offer, and follow based on a humble recognition that they can never be completely certain about what patients most want or need as well as an awareness that wants and needs can change.

How are decisions made about treatment design and delivery?

Health professionals who subscribe to patient-perspective health care provide services based on the priorities and preferences of their patients. Patient-perspective health care professionals are aware of their own scopes of practice and are secure in the knowledge of what they can and cannot offer. A patient-perspective health care system is definitely not a system where "anything goes". Patient-perspective health professionals do not attempt to be all things to all patients. A patient-perspective health system is a system in which health professionals are clear about their roles and are comfortable explaining to patients what they can and cannot provide. Such professionals encourage their patients to think critically about the health information with which they are being presented. They do not feel offended or otherwise slighted if their patients disagree with them, and they don't spend time persuading or otherwise convincing their patients that they should agree with them. Patient-perspective health professionals respectfully assume that their patients are capable of making decisions (after all, they have made countless decisions before accessing the health professional), and they busy themselves with the task of providing the patient with accurate and relevant information. Furthermore, the seeking of other opinions – second, third, and more – is encouraged.

The power imbalance that is often a feature of health care settings was first mentioned in Chapter 2. Patient-perspective health care professionals are attuned to the impact of the power differential that can exist in helping relationships. They realise that patients' words might be used for purposes beyond simply communicating their preferences accurately and assertively. Patients can overtly agree with health professionals when, in fact, they do not concur with the opinions of their treatment provider. Patients might not want to disagree with health professionals for a variety of reasons, so it is important to consider patients' communication holistically and look further than simply attending to the words they utter.

When treatment is discussed, do they seem engaged and interested or have they become distracted or withdrawn? Do they look away as they are talking? Do they give simple, short, abbreviated responses to your questions? Are they late to appointments, or do they not turn up at all? Do they seem overly agreeable?

Compliance and obedience are not considered to be desirable patient attributes in a patient-perspective health care setting. Patients need to be the informed drivers of their health care, not the compliant recipients of the outcomes of other people's deliberations. Patients who do not adhere to the recommendations offered to them are providing health care professionals with important information that could be used to improve the appropriateness of the care being administered.

Engaging or inviting patients

In patient-centred care, part of the common parlance concerns engaging patients in health services. For example, the *National Aboriginal and Torres Strait Islander Health Plan* (Department of Health, 2013a), maintains that "As a mainstream service, *headspace* is ensuring the delivery of culturally appropriate services through an Aboriginal and Torres Strait Islander Strategy Management Committee which provides expert and high level strategic advice on effective mechanisms to engage and meet the needs of Indigenous young people". In this statement, the emphasis is on mechanisms that will engage Indigenous young people and meet their needs. From a patient-perspective approach, however, it is understood that individuals only ever meet their own needs. The responsibility of services and systems lies in providing resources and removing barriers so that an individual's needs fulfilment is more straightforward.

In the *National Framework for Universal Child and Family Health Services* (Department of Health, 2013b), it is stated that "A relationship based on trust and continuity of care is important to engage parents in services, to respond appropriately to parental concerns and to work together towards a common goal". Again, the responsibility is with the service to engage the parents, and while the recommendation to respond appropriately to parental concerns is encouraging, the notion of working together towards a common goal would be out of place in a patient-perspective paradigm. Health professionals in this context, operating from a patient-perspective stance, would work with parents to help the parents achieve their own goals. It is appreciated in patient-perspective health care that goals can never be shared in the same way that one might share a ride with a friend to the beach. Goals are located within the minds of individuals and, as such, the pursuit and actualisation of goals can only ever be experienced individually even though other people, including health professionals, can be essential to ultimately achieving this experience. The discussion regarding shared versus supported decision making in Chapter 3 is relevant here.

In the *Your health. Your say*. (Australian Digital Health Strategy, 2016) discussion paper, the first of three questions being proposed to guide the discussion was: "How do individuals want to engage with digital services to have access to the information they need to improve their health and wellbeing?" (p. 5). The difference in the way "engage" is used here, compared with the previous two examples is, at the same time, both subtle and profound. In this question, the focus is on what individuals want and how services can assist them to get what they want rather than what services will do to individuals. The spirit of this question is clearly aligned with a patient–perspective ethos.

Patient-perspective health professionals persistently and warmly invite patients to make use of the health care resources when and as they need to. The responsibility of a health service, therefore, is to find out what patients want and need and to make resources available to patients so that these goals can be attained. Whether or not patients engage is considered to be the responsibility of the patients but evaluating, in a routine and ongoing manner, the extent to which the service is a service that patients would want to engage with is the remit of a patient–perspective health system.

Managing mistakes and risks

Health professionals in a patient-perspective context manage risks according to their relevant professional and organisational standards. Health professionals with a patient-perspective mindset understand that patients won't always act the way the health professionals think they should. Much of the information already discussed is relevant here. Mistakes and risks will need to be managed in any social system. The way they are managed, however, will depend to a great extent on how they are understood. In a patient-perspective health care system, mistakes and risks are considered in terms of the first-person perspective of the patient. Something that appears to be a mistake to an observer might actually have produced the intended outcome for the person being observed. Similarly, statements or actions that seem to suggest risk to an onlooker might simply be exasperated comments arising from an inability to obtain an effective treatment for the existing ailment. This is not to deny that mistakes and risks exist. It is merely to suggest that the way in which mistakes and risks are defined and then consequently addressed needs to be informed by the first-person perspective of the patient rather than the third-person perspective of a health professional.

Empowering patients

The notion of empowering patients is another oft repeated sentiment within patient-centred care. The suggestion of empowering patients seems to be an antidote to the problematic effects of the power imbalance that often exists in the relationship between a health professional and a patient. Dictionary.com, however, defines "empower" as: "1) to give power or authority to; authorize, especially by legal or official means; 2) to enable or permit". Therefore, empowering seems to be the situation when one person gives power or authority to another person or persons or enables or permits another person or persons to conduct themselves in various ways. Clearly, if someone has the ability or authority to empower, they also have the ability or authority to *dis*empower. So, even in the process of empowering people, the relational power imbalance is preserved.

Rather than empowering, patient-perspective health professionals recognise and endorse the inherent controlling natures of both themselves and their patients (Marken and Carey, 2015). By understanding the implications of these controlling natures, they make efforts to minimise the extent to which they thwart or impede the controlling tendencies of their patients. Moreover, they are clear about their own goals and motives, and they are sensitive to the potential impact they can have in their relationships with patients. They adopt an attitude of service characterised by considered curiosity and following rather than leading. From a control point of view, issues of empowerment become irrelevant, so patient–perspective health professionals are able to focus on different features of their relationships with patients such as the extent to which they are helping or hindering patients in their pursuit of important goals.

Whose standards?

In Chapter 2, I pointed out that, in health care generally, our current predominant focus is about correcting apparent deviations from biological norms. Saini, Garcia-Armesto et al. (2017) claim that this focus is one of the factors that has contributed to the neglect of patient preferences and a lack of patient involvement in decisions about their treatment. A blinkered focus on biological norms is problematic enough; however, the way in which these norms are established is also often contentious. Fundamentally, the concept of "normal" is nebulous and fickle. The kaleidoscopic nature of the concept is particularly evident in relation to health. The World Health Organization (WHO), for example, defines "health" as "a state of complete physical, mental and social well-being and not merely the absence of disease or infirmity" (WHO, 1946). If this definition is to be understood literally, very few people, if anyone, would be considered healthy in any sort of sustained way (Carey, 2016).

The tenuous nature of the definition of health, along with the flexibility of the concept of normal, has enabled people to define and redefine normal for various purposes. Brownlee et al. (2017), for example, report that definitions of disease or abnormality can be broadened so that populations previously considered "normal" are now labelled as ill or unhealthy. This practice has resulted in the overdiagnosis and overmedicalisation of many people. Moynihan and Cassels (2005) provide an example with regard to cholesterol levels of the way in which the diagnostic net can be cast ever more widely so that people who were once considered healthy may now be targeted for unnecessary treatment. The initial demarcation between healthy and unhealthy cholesterol levels meant that 13 million Americans were considered to be in need of treatment (Moynihan and Cassels, 2005). By changing definitions of healthy and unhealthy cholesterol levels, however, this figured increased to 36 million Americans and then to 40 million Americans who were considered to need treatment to reduce their cholesterol levels (Moynihan and Cassels, 2005).

The problems of overdiagnosis and overmedicalisation are particularly problematic when it comes to mental health in which the notion of normal is especially ethereal and the process of diagnosis and treatment can be particularly pernicious. With regard to children, for example, it can be very difficult to diagnose accurately (notwithstanding the debate surrounding the accuracy of psychiatric diagnoses per se) with the result being that children can be labelled and treated unnecessarily (Frances, 2012). Unfortunately, these treatments sometimes have serious side effects and life-altering complications (Frances, 2012).

Ironically, even if we could develop precise and accurate definitions of "normal" and "healthy" that applied cross-culturally, the definitions would not improve the situation greatly. The definitions would still leave unanswered the question of why "normal" should be the standard to which we aspire. And even more importantly, we would still not know whether or not the patients to whom we are offering services *want* to be "normal". Who should decide whether or not a person is normal enough or healthy enough? Rather than a population norm or a health professional's opinion being the decisive element as to whether, how much, and what treatment is provided, the ultimate arbiter of these issues must be the patient. Williams (2015), for example, argues that rather than focussing on narrow definitions of recovery, we need to consider what it means to "be in the world" from the perspective of the patient, which involves not only understanding the individual but also the world and the context within which he lives. Again, by explaining the dynamic interplay between individuals and their environments, PCT provides robust and rigorous principles to understand the phenomena being considered and to plan the most effective ways to assist.

Furthermore, PCT can contribute constructively to the dilemma of what standard to pay attention to and how to use that standard to provide efficient, effective, and appropriate health care. PCT suggests that control rather than health should be the concept we consider when attempting to help people ameliorate problems they are experiencing (Carey, 2016). The important questions, from a PCT perspective, become to what extent are people able to control the things that are important to them, what is interfering with this control, and what help do they need to achieve the control they desire. In a patient-perspective health care system, therefore, health professionals use the standards of individual patients rather than arbitrary population-based norms to guide decisions about appropriate protocols and procedures.

Claire (2007) points out that focussing on what people want and the way in which they are controlling their own lives requires a different kind of contract between health systems and populations than the contract that currently exists. The new contract would be based on assumptions of self-care and personal responsibility nestled within a context of promoting individual control (Claire, 2007). Yet again, the principles of PCT would help to inform the redesign of systems and the ways in which they interact with the populations they have been established to serve.

Applying services or making services available?

Perhaps one of the main distinctions between a patient-centred system and a patient-perspective system is where responsibility for the health of an individual lies. It is implicit in many current initiatives that it is the system's or the service's responsibility to keep individuals healthy. Services, for example, are implored to engage patients in the programs they provide.

Closing the Gap is a national Australian policy to help reduce the disparity in health outcomes between Aboriginal and Torres Strait Islander Australians and their non-Indigenous counterparts. In the latest report, there is an acknowledgement of the need to work with Aboriginal and Torres Strait Islander people and a commitment to accelerate progress so that the seven targets set by the Council of Australian Governments (COAG), which are currently not on track to be achieved, might, eventually, be realised in the timelines specified (Commonwealth of Australia, 2017). In this document, however, there is still a strong sense of the system "doing things to" those people in the population who have been identified as needing correcting. It is stated, for example, that "COAG has reaffirmed that improving the lives of Indigenous Australians is a priority of its strategic forward agenda and agreed that the Closing the Gap framework has played a significant role in driving unprecedented national effort to improve Indigenous outcomes" (p. 7). Here there is a clear indication that COAG has assumed responsibility for improving the lives of Indigenous Australians.

The position of the patient-perspective approach is that it is individuals' responsibility to improve their own lives, and it is a system's or societies' responsibility to ensure they have the resources necessary to do so. This distinction has very important implications when it comes to what we focus our attention on and what we choose to evaluate. If we believe that it is indeed

possible to improve other people's lives and that it is our responsibility to do so, then it is the improvement in their lives that we
will monitor, measure, and report against. On the other hand, if
we understand that it is our responsibility to ensure the necessary resources are in place for people to fashion lives of their
own design, then it is resource allocation we will be monitoring,
measuring, and reporting against. Somewhat paradoxically, the
more we assume responsibility for the conduct of others, the
easier it seems to be to blame these other people when targets
are not reached. A different type of relationship would need to
develop, however, if we focussed on resource provision rather
than other people's conduct. We would need to be informed
by the people we're resourcing as to what resources they need,
when they need them, and in what quantities. We would also
need to check, on an ongoing basis, that the resource supply is
being adequately maintained and that these particular resources
continue to be useful to the people to whom they are being
provided. Health professionals who are committed to a patient-
perspective way of working, therefore, promote the availability
of health services to patients to enable patients to achieve the
goals they seek to experience.

Concluding comments

While the impact of the patient-perspective ethos is profound and
far reaching, it is, simultaneously, quite straightforward. There are
implications, however, for policy, practice, and research, as well as
education and training. The overriding lesson is that patients need
to be the drivers of decisions regarding the development and delivery of health services. To re-position patients in this way, we will
need to regard patients as capable and competent decision makers
who are able to determine what they need as well as when they
need it and when they no longer need it. For some health professionals, this will be entirely consistent with the way they already

practice. For other health professionals, however, the approach required by a patient-perspective mandate will be confronting. The next chapter provides an illustration of the patient-perspective approach with regard to the scheduling of appointments for psychological treatment. In many ways, appointment scheduling should be a benign example holding little, if any interest. As it has transpired, however, the issue of how and when appointments for psychological treatment should be scheduled highlights many of the issues raised in this chapter and continues to be contentious.

References

American Psychological Association (APA). (2017). *Ethical principles of psychologists and code of conduct.* Washington, DC: Author.

Australian Digital Health Strategy. (2016). *Your health. Your say. Shaping the future of health and care together. A consultation with the Australian community to co-produce the National Digital Health Strategy: Discussion paper.* Retrieved June 17, 2017, from https://conversation.digitalhealth.gov.au/sites/default/files/PDF/Your%20health.%20Your%20say.%20Discussion%20Paper.pdf

Australian Health Ministers' Advisory Council. (2013). *A national framework for recovery-oriented mental health services: Guide for practitioners and providers.* Canberra, ACT: Commonwealth of Australia. Retrieved June 12, 2017, from www.health.gov.au/internet/main/publishing.nsf/content/67D17065514 CF8E8CA257C1D00017A90/$File/recovgde.pdf

Australian Psychological Society. (2007). *Code of ethics.* Melbourne, VIC: Author.

British Psychological Society. (2009). *Code of ethics and conduct.* Leicester: Author.

Brownlee, S., Chalkidou, K., Doust, J., Elshaug, A. G., Glasziou, P., Heath, I., . . . Korenstein, D. (2017). Evidence for overuse of medical services around the world. *Lancet,* Published online 8 January. http://dx.doi.org/10.1016/S0140-6736(16)32585-5

Canadian Psychological Association. (2000). *Canadian code of ethics for psychologists* (3rd ed.). Ottawa: Author.

Carey, T. A. (2016). Health is control. *Annals of Behavioural Science, 2*(1), 1–3.

Claire, A. (2007). Mental health. Time to step up to patient-centred care. *Health Service Journal, 117*(6072), 16–17.

Commonwealth of Australia. (2017). *Closing the gap Prime Minister's report 2017.* Canberra: Author. Retrieved June 18, 2017, from http://closingthegap.pmc.gov.au/sites/default/files/ctg-report-2017.pdf

Department of Health. (2013a). *National aboriginal and Torres Strait Islander health plan: Companion document on Commonwealth Government strategies and reforms*. Retrieved June 17, 2017, from www.health.gov.au/internet/publications/publishing.nsf/ Content/natsihp-companion-toc~invest-outcomes~adolescence-develop

Department of Health. (2013b). *National framework for universal child and family health services*. Retrieved June 17, 2017, from www.health.gov.au/ internet/publications/publishing.nsf/Content/nat-fram-ucfhs-html~ framework~health-development

Frances, A. (2012). Better safe than sorry. *Australian and New Zealand Journal of Psychiatry, 46*(8), 695–696.

Griffith, G. M., Hutchinson, L., & Hastings, R. P. (2013). "I'm not a patient, I'm a person": The experiences of individuals with intellectual disabilities and challenging behavior – a thematic synthesis of qualitative studies. *Clinical Psychology: Science and Practice, 20*(4), 469–488.

Jachuck, S. J., Brierley, H., Jachuck, S., & Willcox, P. M. (1982). The effect of hypotensive drugs on the quality of life. *Journal of the Royal College of General Practitioners, 32*, 103–105.

Marken, R. S., & Carey, T. A. (2015). *Controlling people: The paradoxical nature of being human*. Brisbane: Australian Academic Press.

Moynihan, R., & Cassels, A. (2005). *Selling sickness: How the world's biggest pharmaceutical companies are turning us all into patients*. New York: Nation Books.

Robertson, R. J., & Powers, W. T. (1990). *Introduction to modern psychology: The control theory view*. Gravel Switch, KY: Control Systems Group.

Saini, V., Garcia-Armesto, S., Klemperer, D., Paris, V., Elshaug, A. G., Brownlee, S., . . . Fisher, E. S. (2017). *Drivers of poor medical care*. Lancet, Published online 8 January. http://dx.doi.org/10.1016/S0140-6736(16)30947-3

Syme, S. L. (2004). Social determinants of health: The community as empowered partner. *Preventing Chronic Disease: Public Health Research, Practice, and Policy, 1*(1), 1–5.

Velmans, M. (2009). *Understanding consciousness* (2nd ed.). London: Routledge.

Victorian Government Department of Health. (2013). *National practice standards for the mental health workforce*. Melbourne, VIC: Author. Retrieved June 14, 2017, from www.health.gov.au/internet/main/publishing.nsf/content/ 5D7909E82304E6D2CA257C430004E877/$File/wkstd13.pdf

WHO. (1946). *Constitution of the World Health Organization*. Geneva: Author. Retrieved June 18, 2017, from http://apps.who.int/gb/bd/PDF/bd47/ EN/constitution-en.pdf?ua=1

Williams, C. H. (2015). Improving access to psychological therapies (IAPT) and treatment outcomes: Epistemological assumptions and controversies. *Journal of Psychiatric & Mental Health Nursing, 22*(5), 344–351.

7

PATIENT-LED APPOINTMENT SCHEDULING

A PRACTICAL EXAMPLE OF PATIENT-PERSPECTIVE CARE

The previous chapter outlined in a general sense some of the implications for health service provision of applying the principles of patient-perspective care. In this chapter, I will further illustrate the application of patient-perspective principles with a specific example from my clinical work in both the United Kingdom and Australia. The example concerns the very routine matter of the way in which appointments are scheduled for the provision of psychological treatment. Despite the mundane nature of this topic, it appears to be the case that the way in which appointments are scheduled can have dramatic effects on service capacity, waiting times, appointment attendance, and access to services.

The problem with missed appointments

The frequent and costly nature of missed appointments in health care was first mentioned in Chapters 3 and 4. It was also highlighted in Chapter 3 that there is a significant disconnect between how long we design treatments to be and how long patients *want* treatments to be as evidenced by the number of appointments they attend in routine clinical practice. Both these issues are addressed with a patient-led approach to appointment scheduling.

Kheirkhah, Feng, Travis, Tavakoli-Tabasi, and Sharafkhaneh (2016) describe the non-attendance of patients at scheduled appointments as a major obstacle to cost-effective health care as well as patient safety. In Chapter 4, for example, it was mentioned that Gbolade (2010) reported an estimated annual figure of approximately £600 million being the amount of revenue that is lost each year in the United Kingdom's National Health Service (NHS) due to missed appointments. Not only is this problem costly, but it is also long-standing. Stone, Palmer, Saxby, and Devaraj (1999), for example, reported that missed appointments cost the NHS £266 million in 1984, and £360 million was being wasted annually at the time their paper was published 15 years later.

Trying to remedy the situation

Various initiatives have been introduced to reduce the number of missed appointments including SMS text messages and reminder phone calls. In their retrospective cohort study, however, Kheirkhah et al. (2016) reported that the no show rate did not change after implementing a reminder system. Similarly, Clough and Casey (2014) conducted a randomised controlled trial to compare the effect of receiving appointment reminders by SMS text messages with not receiving the reminders. They found that there were no significant differences between the SMS and no SMS groups with regard to appointment attendance. The SMS group, however, had *more* treatment dropouts compared with the no SMS group. A strategy that appears to have been neglected, is to change the appointment scheduling system itself. Marshall's et al. (2015) identification of the rigidity of services and their lack of flexibility in managing individual needs and preferences as major barriers to attendance mentioned in Chapter 3 is evidence of the need for system reform.

Getting interested in appointment scheduling

With regard to the provision of psychological treatment, the standard way of scheduling appointments is for the treatment provider to suggest a suitable protocol of appointment frequency and duration. Appointments are typically booked in a regular pattern occurring every week or every two weeks with the frequency being decreased by increasing the intervals between appointments as the treatment provider determines that the patient is progressing satisfactorily. There is compelling evidence, however, that patients prefer a variable schedule of appointment attendance as well as, typically, attending fewer sessions than treatment providers expect them to attend.

I didn't ever anticipate becoming interested in something as seemingly innocuous as the scheduling of appointments. Yet events transpired such that this area became a major focus of my research. After completing my PhD in Australia, I spent five years working in the NHS in Scotland. I worked in the adult primary care service of a large clinical psychology department. When I first arrived, there was a 15-month waiting list in our service to see a psychologist. This meant that if someone was referred in March of one year by her general practitioner (GP) to see a psychologist, she could expect to receive a letter advising her of the time and date of her first appointment in June *of the following year*. Perhaps unsurprisingly, of the first people with whom I arranged appointments, two of them couldn't remember why they had been referred, but it had taken them so long to get an appointment that they were adamant they were going to keep it. Given this state of affairs, it was also unsurprising that there were clear and explicit NHS policy statements in areas such as improving access to services and giving patients greater choice and control over their health care (Carey and Spratt, 2009).

It wasn't the length of the waiting list or the policy directives, however, that piqued my interest in this area. Rather, during my first two weeks in my new position, I met various people and received a range of information about different aspects of my role. In this orientation period, my supervisor informed me that in this service, it was the standard practice to schedule appointments every two weeks. I was surprised at this because in Australia, I had been used to scheduling weekly appointments. I began to wonder what the rationale was for either weekly or biweekly appointments.

Looking for the evidence

Because I had just completed my PhD, I was accustomed to consulting the literature when I wanted information on a topic, so, in this instance, I again turned to journals and books. I began to scour databases for published, credible information that would provide an answer to the reason why we schedule appointments the way that we do. As I was exploring this area, I also became interested in why we developed treatments of a specified number of sessions. I wasn't necessarily interested in the number of sessions of any particular treatment; instead, I was intrigued as to how the numbers in general were derived. Again, I wanted to know what the rationale was for a particular treatment length. For a 12-session treatment of cognitive behaviour therapy (CBT), for example, where did the number 12 come from? Furthermore, how was the notion of a 50-minute treatment session established? I came to realise that these are important questions with profound implications for services. If, for example, we discovered that a treatment program of four sessions lasting 30 minutes each was effective in reducing psychological distress and restoring contentment and satisfaction, that would have significantly different resourcing implications from a 12-session treatment program with 50-minute sessions.

I discovered in my review of the literature that there was no shortage of studies comparing treatments of different length. I obtained studies, for example, comparing one session with five sessions and eight sessions with 16 sessions (Carey, 2005). What I could not find, however, was any rationale for why the numbers one, five, eight, and 16 had been selected (Carey, 2005). A key insight occurred to me as I was devouring this literature. I realised that a study demonstrating that 12 sessions of a particular treatment was effective, relative to a comparison group, in helping to reduce symptoms of psychological distress was *not* a study demonstrating that 12 sessions were *necessary* for reducing psychological distress. Again, the importance of distinguishing between what is possible and what is necessary is important here. The distinction between necessary and possible is a crucial point but one that seems to have been overlooked by policymakers, health service managers, and service providers.

There is good evidence that we are currently overtreating people accessing psychological treatments. Or, at least, we endeavour to overtreat. As mentioned earlier, treatments are generally developed to be greater than ten sessions long; however, patients in routine clinical practice, on average, attend less than ten sessions (Carey, 2011).

Perhaps the disjuncture between how long therapists think treatments should be and how long patients attend treatment for has arisen because there has never been any empirical investigations to establish what an appropriate treatment length might be. Perry (1987), for example, maintains that the decisions about session frequency are based on tradition, logistics, and clinical experience rather than systematic research. Haley (1990) suggested that "The ideology and practice of therapy was largely determined when therapists chose to sit with a client and be paid for durations of time rather than by results" (p. 15). How delicious it is to think of what the practice of delivering psychotherapy might look like if people paid us for results rather than time! Of most interest, however, may be the fact that, when it comes to treatment effectiveness, length of treatment doesn't seem to matter. Lambert (2007) reported that treatment length is relatively unimportant to positive outcomes for patients. This statement echoes a conclusion offered by Perry (1987) who, 20 years earlier, had suggested that comparative studies generally fail to demonstrate a significant advantage of longer treatment.

The beginnings of the system

Given that there was no compelling guidance in the literature for any particular treatment length nor any ideal schedule of treatment sessions, I wondered what would transpire if patients, rather than therapists, determined the length and frequency of treatment provision. I began to establish procedures for patients to schedule appointments according to their own preferences rather than therapists advising patients when they should attend. The system was developed and first evaluated in the NHS (Carey, 2005) in which patients are referred for psychological treatment by their GP. At the first appointment of psychological treatment, it was explained to patients the way in which they could schedule appointments. Essentially, patient appointment scheduling involved nothing more complex than the patient contacting the practice receptionist in the same way they would to schedule an appointment with a GP.

Continuing the search for a rationale

As I developed this system and began evaluating it, I continued to explore the way in which we might have arrived at our current situation of treatment structure and delivery. I emailed leaders in the field and asked them if they knew "of any details about how and where the idea of weekly treatment sessions for 16 or so weeks developed?". Aaron T. Beck replied: "The 16 weeks was based on clinical experience" (personal communication, 29 October 2009). Isaac Marks commented: "I don't know. Different authors used frequencies of treatment sessions that varied (and still vary) greatly from daily to weekly or less often, with session durations varying from 50' to several hours, and total treatment period from just one session to even longer than 16 weeks, depending on the method used and problem treated" (personal communication, 27 October 2009). As is demonstrated in Table 7.1, Marks was accurate in his summary of the situation. In the 1970s when highly regarded treatments such as CBT were being established, there was a tremendous amount of variability of session duration and frequency. The list in Table 7.1 is, undoubtedly, not exhaustive, but it serves to highlight the lack of standardisation that existed in today's ancestral treatments. Of particular note is that, again, rationales were not provided for the decisions regarding the durations and frequencies specified.

Developing the program

As I continued to introduce the patient-led approach to appointment scheduling into the clinics where I worked, a small number of colleagues became interested in this approach and adopted the system as their own. We were also using an a-diagnostic cognitive therapy called the Method of Levels (MOL; Carey, 2006; 2008; Carey, Mansell, and Tai, 2015; Mansell, Carey, and Tai, 2012), which was ideally suited to the patient-led approach to appointment scheduling. MOL is a flexible and responsive cognitive therapy that focusses on the perspective of the patient and encourages patients to describe their perspectives and explore them in detail.

Table 7.1 Early studies of psychological treatment reporting durations and frequencies of treatment.

Format	Therapy	Reference	Duration	Frequency
Individual	Imaginal flooding vs supportive therapy vs no treatment	Hannie & Adams (1974)	At least nine sessions	Three times a week
Individual	Functional problem-solving vs "support only" vs waiting list	Shipley and Fazio (1973)	Three weeks	Weekly
Couples	Social-skills behaviour therapy vs "doctor's choice"	McLean, Ogston and Grauer (1973)	Eight weeks	Weekly
Couples	Social-skills behaviour therapy vs dynamically oriented psychotherapy vs tricyclic pharmacotherapy vs progressive muscle relaxation therapy	McLean and Hakstian (1979)	Ten weeks	Weekly
Group	Self-control cognitive-behaviour therapy vs non-specific treatment vs waiting list	Fuchs and Rehm (1977)	Six weeks	Weekly
Individual	Cognitive therapy vs tricyclic antidepressant	Rush, Beck, Kovacs and Hollon (1977) [cited in Kovacs (1979)]	A maximum of 20 sessions over 12 weeks	Unspecified
Group	Cognitive therapy vs social-skills therapy	Shaw (1977)	Four two-hour sessions	Weekly

(*Continued*)

Table 7.1 (Continued)

Format	Therapy	Reference	Duration	Frequency
Individual	Cognitive therapy vs behaviour therapy vs cognitive behaviour therapy	Taylor and Marshall (1977) [cited in Kovacs (1979)]	Six sessions	Unspecified
Individual	Cognitive therapy vs behaviour therapy vs cognitive behaviour therapy vs waiting list	Taylor (1974)	Three weeks	Twice weekly
Individual	Cognitive therapy	Shaw (1974)	Ten sessions	Twice weekly
Individual	Cognitive therapy vs behaviour therapy vs non-directive therapy vs waiting list	Shaw (1975)	Eight two-hour sessions	Twice weekly
Individual	Cognitive therapy	Beck (1976)	A maximum of 20 sessions in a maximum of 20 weeks	Unspecified
Individual	Cognitive therapy	Beck (1976)	A maximum of 12 weeks	Twice weekly
Individual	Rational vs psychoanalytically oriented psychotherapy vs orthodox psychoanalysis	Ellis (1957)	The rational therapy group left treatment after an average of 26 sessions; the psychoanalytically oriented psychotherapy group left treatment after an average of 35 sessions; the orthodox psychoanalysis group left therapy after an average of 93 sessions	Unspecified

Format	Therapy	Reference	Duration	Frequency
Individual	Cognitive behavioural therapy	Rush, Khatami and Beck (1975)	Cases 1–12, sessions over four months; cases 2–20, sessions over five months; all cases, 3–5 sessions	Case 1, weekly, then biweekly, then monthly sessions; case 2, weekly sessions for three months; biweekly for two months; case 3, weekly sessions

The program continued for the five years that I worked in the NHS in Scotland, and when I operated a psychology clinic in the public mental health service of Alice Springs, I used the same system of appointment scheduling (Carey, Tai, and Stiles, 2013). During the time the patient-led system has been used, various evaluations have been conducted with the results being published as peer-reviewed publications and presented at conferences. As will be explained later, the approach has been highly successful in reducing missed appointments and improving access to services, but, curiously, it has not been enthusiastically embraced in any sort of large-scale way by clinicians and health service managers.

Results and conclusions

Despite the misgivings of some of our colleagues about the ability of patients to use this system, the patient-led approach to appointment scheduling has been demonstrated to be highly effective across different practices, in different health services, in different countries, with different therapists, and across primary and secondary care services (Carey, 2010; 2011; Carey and Mullan, 2007; Carey and Spratt, 2009; Carey et al., 2013). It requires no additional resources in terms of finances, personnel, or time. Sending out reminders to patients, for example, requires someone to send them out or to monitor that they have been sent out.

Although only a small number of clinicians were using this approach to appointment scheduling, it had a substantial impact on waiting times in the service where it was first developed. The waiting list had been reduced from 15 months when I first started working in this particular service to less than one month when I left almost five years later. Primarily, the success of this program seemed to be achieved through a reduction in the number of missed and cancelled appointments. Across all of the evaluations, the median number of missed appointments was routinely zero (e.g., Carey and Mullan, 2007; Carey and Spratt, 2009). One study demonstrated a reduction in the number of missed appointments for the first appointment scheduled (Carey and Kemp, 2007). Another study reported an increase in referrals from 52 in one six-month period to 93 in the same six-month period of the following year at the same time as the eradication of a seven-month waiting (Carey and Spratt, 2009). The only change that was made in this study was the way in which appointments were scheduled. To remove a seven-month waiting list and almost double the referral capacity of a service through the seemingly trivial change of shifting appointment booking responsibilities from clinicians to patients is extraordinary. In addition to a reduction in missed appointments, patients demonstrated positive clinical outcomes with only a small average number of scheduled appointments (e.g., Carey et al., 2013).

In the context of the simplicity of this system along with the many positive features it seems to reflect, it is somewhat mind-boggling that clinicians, policymakers, and health service managers are not clamouring for this technology. In general, there has been a steadfast reluctance to adopt this approach. One student

even had to change his PhD topic because he was initially interested in comparing patient-led appointment scheduling with
conventional appointment scheduling but, after almost two years
of approaching many services and having the idea rejected, he
was in danger of not being able to complete his PhD if he persisted with this topic. Perhaps this is another example of how
dangerous the patient–perspective idea is.

It may be that this failure to institute patient-led appoint
scheduling is a sign of how far out of reach the patient-
perspective approach currently is for many health professionals.
Fundamentally, this approach insists on optimistically respect-
ing a patient's ability to make the right decision. And "right"
is, of course, defined from the patient's perspective. Could this
system also possibly reveal an unconscious stigma that health
professionals have regarding people identified as having "mental
health problems"? Would we feel more comfortable entrusting
someone who was diagnosed with stage II pancreatic cancer to
make his own appointments than we would someone who was
diagnosed with social phobia? Whatever the reasons, the story
so far of patient-led appointment scheduling provides a sombre
tale of how difficult it might be to establish a patient–perspective
approach to health care on a widespread scale despite the benefits it affords in the provision of appropriate care.

References

Beck, A. T. (1976). *Cognitive therapy and the emotional disorders*. New York: International Universities Press, Inc.

Carey, T. A. (2005). Can patients specify treatment parameters? A preliminary
investigation. *Clinical Psychology and Psychotherapy, 12,* 326–335.

Carey, T. A. (2006). *The method of levels: How to do psychotherapy without getting in
the way*. Hayward, CA: Living Control Systems Publishing.

Carey, T. A. (2008). *Hold that thought! Two steps to effective counseling and psychotherapy with the Method of Levels*. Chapel Hill, NC: Newview Publications.

Carey, T. A. (2010). Will you follow while they lead? Introducing a patient-
led approach to low intensity CBT interventions. In J. Bennett-Levy et al.

(Eds.), *Oxford guide to low intensity CBT interventions* (pp. 331–338). Oxford: Oxford University Press.

Carey, T. A. (2011). As you like it: Adopting a patient-led approach to psychological treatments. *Journal of Public Mental Health, 10*(1), 6–16.

Carey, T. A., & Kemp, K. (2007). Self selecting first appointments: A replication and consideration of the implications for patient-centred care. *Clinical Psychology Forum, 178,* 33–36.

Carey, T. A., Mansell, W., & Tai, S. J. (2015). *Principles-based counselling and psychotherapy: A method of levels approach.* London: Routledge.

Carey, T. A., & Mullan, R. J. (2007). Patients taking the lead: A naturalistic investigation of a patient led approach to treatment in primary care. *Counselling Psychology Quarterly, 20*(1), 27–40.

Carey, T. A., & Spratt, M. B. (2009). When is enough enough? Structuring the organization of treatment to maximise patient choice and control. *The Cognitive Behaviour Therapist, 2,* 211–226.

Carey, T. A., Tai, S. J., & Stiles, W. B. (2013). Effective and efficient: Using patient-led appointment scheduling in routine mental health practice in remote Australia. *Professional Psychology: Research and Practice, 44,* 405–414.

Clough, B. A., & Casey, L. M. (2014). Using SMS reminders in psychology clinics: A cautionary tale. *Behavioural and Cognitive Psychotherapy, 42,* 257–268.

Ellis, A. (1957). Outcome of employing three different techniques of psychotherapy. *Journal of Clinical Psychology, 13,* 344–350.

Fuchs, C. Z., & Rehm, L. P. (1977). A self-control behavior therapy program for depression. *Journal of Consulting and Clinical Psychology, 45,* 206–215.

Gbolade, B. A. (2010). A snap audit of "did not attend" patients in a gynecologic outpatient clinic. *Clinical Audit, 2,* 93–96.

Haley, J. (1990). Why not long-term therapy? In J. K. Zeig and S. G. Gilligan (Eds.), *Brief therapy: Myths, methods, and metaphors* (pp. 3–17). New York: Brunner/Mazel.

Hannie, T. J., & Adams, H. E. (1974). Modification of agitated depression by flooding: A preliminary study. *Journal of Behavior Therapy and Experimental Psychiatry, 5,* 161–166.

Kheirkhah, P., Feng, Q., Travis, L. M., Tavakoli-Tabasi, S., & Sharafkhaneh, A. (2016). Prevalence, predictors and economic consequences of no-shows. *BMC Health Services Research, 16*(13), 1–6. doi:10.1186/s12913-015-1243-z

Kovacs, M. (1979). Treating depressive disorders: The efficacy of behaviour and cognitive therapies. *Behavior Modification, 3*(4), 496–517.

Lambert, M. (2007). Presidential address: What have we learned from a decade of research aimed at improving psychotherapy outcome in routine care. *Psychotherapy Research, 17*(1), 1–14.

Mansell, W., Carey, T. A., & Tai, S. J. (2012). *A transdiagnostic approach to CBT using method of levels therapy: Distinctive features*. London: Routledge. ISBN: 978-0-415-50764-6

Marshall, D., Quinn, C., Child, S., Shenton, D., Pooler, J., Forber, S., & Byng, R. (2015). What IAPT services can learn from those who do not attend. *Journal of Mental Health, 25*(5), 410–415.

McLean, P. D., & Hakstian, A. R. (1979). Clinical depression: Comparative efficacy of outpatient treatments. *Journal of Consulting and Clinical Psychology, 47*(5), 818–836.

McLean, P. D., Ogston, K., & Grauer, L. (1973). A behavioral approach to the treatment of depression. *Journal of Behavior Therapy and Experimental Psychiatry, 4,* 323–330.

Perry, S. (1987). The choice of duration and frequency of outpatient psychotherapy. In R. E. Hales and A. J. Frances (Eds.), *Annual review* (vol. 6, pp. 398–414). Washington, DC: American Psychiatric Association.

Rush, A. J., Beck, A. T., Kovacs, M., & Hollon, S. (1977). Comparative efficacy of cognitive therapy and pharmacotherapy in the treatment of depressed outpatients. *Cognitive Therapy and Research, 1,* 17–37.

Rush, A. J., Khatami, M., & Beck, A. T. (1975). Cognitive and behavior therapy in chronic depression. *Behavior Therapy, 6*(3), 398–404.

Shaw, B. F. (1974). *Outpatient cognitive therapy of depression*. Unpublished study.

Shaw, B. F. (1975). *A systematic investigation of three treatments of depression*. Doctoral Dissertation. London, University of Western Ontario.

Shaw, B. F. (1977). Comparison of cognitive therapy and behaviour therapy in the treatment of depression. *Journal of Consulting and Clinical Psychology, 45,* 543-51.

Shipley, C. R., & Fazio, A. F. (1973). Pilot study of a treatment for psychological depression. *Journal of Abnormal Psychology, 82,* 372–376.

Stone, C., Palmer, J., Saxby, P., & Devaraj, V. S. (1999). Reducing nonattendance at outpatient clinics. *Journal of the Royal Society of Medicine, 92,* 114–118.

Taylor, F. G. (1974). *Cognitive and behavioral approaches to the modification of depression*. Doctoral dissertation. Queen's University, Kinston, Ontario.

8

PATIENTS' PERSPECTIVES

A book about the patient-perspective approach to health care would be incomplete without including a chapter of patients' experiences of health services from their points of view. In this chapter, a small number of people who have been patients, or the carers and advocates of patients, provide examples of their journey through a health system in which their views were not sought or respected and in which their perspectives were not used to inform treatment design and delivery. These people each have unique stories about different aspects of health care. Their accounts are compelling and provide a potent justification for the urgency of converting to a patient-perspective model of health service delivery.

In preparing their stories, some people asked for a guide as to how their writing should be structured, so I suggested four questions that could be considered. These were the questions people kept in mind as they described their experiences:

1. Can you think of a time when you received less than ideal care from a health professional?
2. What was it about the care that made it less than ideal?
3. How could it have been improved?
4. What would you most like health professionals to know or do?

The stories come from Bronwyn, Davey (told by his dad and mum), Jasmine, Alex (told by his mum), and Donna. The names Davey and Alex are pseudonyms because these people are children, but all the other details about their stories are accurate (Davey's mum's and dad's names are pseudonyms, too). In various ways, all the stories illustrate less than appropriate health care. The inappropriate care that was received differs in its seriousness and severity, and at times, in the midst of the inappropriate care, there were sensitive and caring health professionals. While the contribution of these health professionals should not be discounted, neither should their efforts divert our attention from the overall problem of care that is delivered without considering the priorities, preferences, and values of the individual patient to whom it is being delivered.

Bronwyn is in her mid-40s. She has been married for 20 years and has a daughter who is nine years old. She has a bachelor's degree in commerce but has never used the degree. Recently, Bronwyn studied for and obtained a certificate in disability, and she is now pursuing a career working with people with disabilities. She also has plans to complete a certificate in mental health to help her get a job when she and her family finally leave Alice Springs. Over the past 20 years, Bronwyn has lived in rural and remote locations in Queensland, the Northern Territory, and Western Australia, including Mount Isa and Alice Springs.

Davey's story in this book is told by his dad (John) with his mum (Ann) providing details and edits as required. Davey is a bright, articulate 10-year-old boy who enjoys building with Legos, playing Minecraft and Roblox, watching YouTube, and watching movies with his mother and father. He especially likes sitting in the front row at the cinema. He can run 10 km in under an hour and wants to break world records when he grows up. Two of his favourite subjects at school are maths and science, but he particularly loves PE (physical education).

Jasmine is a 24-year-old artist and mental health advocate living and practising in Manchester in the northwest of England. She was brought up in south-east London by her mother. From a generational line of outspoken feminists and activists, the importance of being vocal in the face of social injustice, fighting with voice and pen to make a positive change in the world, to never bowing down in times of hardship, and to never ever settle for being good at something ". . . for a girl" were instilled in her from a very young age alongside a distinct distrust of authority. Art has been as a means of self-expression and self-directed therapy for Jasmine since infancy, and she prides herself on a large collection of curiosities that she has amassed since then, which both inspire and influence her art. Her family nurtured her creativity fiercely, and she has kept sketchbooks since she was 5. Having volunteered in the areas of criminal justice and mental health since the age of 17, Jasmine believes strongly in a complete reform of the education, prison, and mental health infrastructure to achieve an inclusive, compassionate, and progressive society. Jasmine is happiest when with her sisterhood, whether they be sitting at home with her cat Chubba, scouring charity shops for treasure, or exploring forests. Jasmine's one true love is swimming outdoors in all weathers. Fascinated by fairy tales and folklore, Jasmine hopes to one day be remembered as a storyteller, if nothing else.

Alex's mum tells his story in this book, which, in a way, is her story, too. It's the story of a parent trying desperately to do the right thing and do what is best for her son but having to navigate confusing, and sometimes unhelpful, health and education systems to do so. Alex is a smart and delightful 6-year-old boy who lives with his mother, father, and older brother in the northern suburbs of Brisbane, Queensland (QLD). He is tall for his age, so lots of people frequently think he's older than he is. Alex learns quickly and often surprises people with how much he knows because he doesn't always appear to be listening to what is being said. He is remarkably independent and can engage in the activities he enjoys for long periods of time. Through his cheerful and quirky nature, Alex provides a very important and powerful reminder to those who know him of the dangers in having a narrow idea of what "normal" is or should be. He demonstrates how much nicer the world is when difference is celebrated, respected, and encouraged. People shouldn't be forced to fit into a mould but will develop in their own way and at their own pace if they are supported to do so.

Donna is a 49-year-old Aboriginal woman who identifies as Wakaya, Jaru, and Bunuba and lives in Halls Creek, Western Australia (WA). She grew up in North West Queensland but for most of her adult life has lived in the Barkly and Central regions of the Northern Territory as well as in the Kimberley region of WA. Donna has worked in the areas of health, employment, Social and Emotional Wellbeing, legal services, drug and alcohol, and domestic violence and child safety. She is currently employed as a project officer with the Kimberley Language Resource Centre in Halls Creek. Donna has 30 years of experience working with and advocating for Australian Indigenous people who mostly live in remote locations. She sees community people as the "experts" and the qualified people as the "professionals", and she maintains that to get outcomes with and for Aboriginal and Torres Strait Islander people, the experts and the professionals need to be respected on the same level and be treated accordingly.

Bronwyn's story

My life with mental illness started 20 years ago. I had been diagnosed with Depression and knew very little about what it all meant. My GP at the time suggested a counsellor who I saw once a fortnight. I found these sessions helpful but I didn't keep them up after moving away with my boyfriend to another town and then found myself on return to the same GP with my medication increased. Years later I found out that increasing this particular medication can bring on psychotic episodes and that's exactly what happened. I ended up in a psychiatric ward for the first time in my life. I was very scared and confused. I was hospitalised for six weeks and was discharged with the diagnosis of schizophrenia even though I went in to hospital with a diagnosis of depression. While I was in hospital I was never formally interviewed or asked whether I ever heard voices. I knew very little about this most recent diagnosis but after attending some "Grow" meetings which the hospital recommended I realised what schizophrenia meant. I didn't attend the meetings anymore and stopped taking the one tablet the hospital had had me on.

I went five years without medication until, while I was on holidays, I had another psychotic episode. This time the hospital diagnosed me with Bipolar Depression. I myself realised that I needed medication but I did not accept that I had Bipolar. Again I was never formally interviewed or spoken to. I was scripted an anti-depressant and an anti-psychotic. I took them both religiously for ten years. In that time I was hospitalised several times for psychotic episodes but never for my depression. I tried to get myself some help but living in a regional area did not leave me with a lot of options. There was a psychiatrist who visited the town once a month. I saw this psychiatrist and I also saw a psychologist. I thought the psychologist would help me come to terms with the sexual abuse that I had suffered as a child and had recently started remembering but he was more interested in the next job he had applied for. He let me pour my heart and my emotions out to him but never gave me any counselling or coping skills. He told me that he had a new job working with Aboriginal people that he was going to and he could not help me. I felt very deflated and lost.

It wasn't until 2007 that my diagnosis was the correct one and that was Depression and Post Traumatic Stress Disorder. I had my daughter in 2008 knowing it was safe on the medication I was on and that is when things really unravelled. The abuse came back with a vengeance and I was also remembering the babies I had lost years earlier. Even though I was cleared by the psychiatrist in the week I was in hospital with my daughter I was hospitalised again for Post Natal Depression. I believe my problems at the time had nothing to do with Post Natal Depression and everything to do with my abuse and loss. If I could have had counselling instead of being hospitalised all the time I believe my problems would have been addressed a lot better. This continued on for four more years with the worst treatment happening later.

During my worst period of hospitalisation I was subjected to medication changes so that I was no longer taking the medication that had been working for me effectively and I was diagnosed with Schizo Affective Disorder. The psychiatrist at the time not once asked me what was troubling me and did not listen to my constant requests to go home and be with my daughter. He made me an involuntary patient several times and even ordered me to have electric shock treatment. Thankfully another psychiatrist took over at that time and found me not suitable for that treatment. Meantime I was scared, fretting about my daughter, and feeling like no one really cared, especially the psychiatrist. For no good reason I was hospitalised for a six-month period and had to endure a lot of heartache. I was not treated as a mother by the psychiatrist and no discussion was held about what had already been achieved by my previous hospital visit in Perth. I lost six months with my daughter and husband and I can never get that back.

My last hospitalisation was nearly four years ago and I have made a conscious effort to stay well. There is another point I would like to make in that medication changes are not always the answer. This can be illustrated by an overdose in 2013 where I had been taken off my new anti-depressant which was working and my new anti-psychotic and put on some older forms of medication. I have researched the older medication since that time and found that it can cause suicidal tendencies. Although I was very unhappy in my relationship and I believe marriage counselling was the answer in hindsight, the older medication made me very unstable. I would love to make the psychiatrist who treated me this way accountable for the decisions he made as I feel it was his decisions that were responsible for me feeling the way that I did. But in reality, accountability like that does not happen in the mental health system. After my overdose and hospitalisation my new anti-depressant was given to me once more with some extra new medication.

It took about a year to get over the overdose happening and then I started seeing a good psychologist who worked through my loss and sexual abuse. After about two years I got my Post Traumatic Stress under control. Now I am not haunted by daily flashbacks and I have slowly come to terms with the loss of my babies.

I believe if the system is going to change it has to come from within. The attitudes of mental health professionals towards the mentally ill have to change. It is not as simple as popping a pill to change the serotonin level in the brain. It is about dealing with personal issues and getting the right psychological support to dig deeper to solve the underlying cause. It has to be determined by a dedicated team and it has to be able to be long term. Until this happens there will continue to be long term suffering and a revolving door to the hospital system. I also believe learning to manage stress levels would help and mental health workers should not put all mental health patients in one basket.

Davey's story

The first nine months of Davey's life were idyllic. As far as we could tell he was as happy and content as any developing life could be. His mum did what she could, through diet, exercise, and lifestyle in general, to nurture and protect the environment in which he was growing and developing. Davey's arrival into the space where both me and his mum could hold him, watch him, listen to him, snuggle him, and so on was perhaps the most profoundly joyous moment of my life.

We were particularly pleased, at least initially, with the standard of care we had received before and during Davey's birth. Furthermore, we saw encouraging signs around the maternity hospital where Ann and Davey spent the first ten days of Davey's life "on the outside". There were posters around the hospital, for example, promoting a "feeding on demand" attitude to breastfeeding. As events unfolded, however, it became apparent that the staff didn't seem to pay as much attention to the posters as we had.

Although Davey's birthing had proceeded "naturally" at first, as he got closer and closer to experiencing first-hand the sights and sounds of the hospital environment, it became clear that the size of Davey's head and the size of Ann's pelvis necessitated a change of strategy. The final stage of Davey's arrival was facilitated by an emergency caesarean operation in the early hours of a winter's night. After the marathon effort involved in transitioning Davey from inside to outside, both Ann and Davey managed to sleep for the few hours of darkness that remained.

It was after Davey's birth that the inappropriate care commenced. For reasons that were never revealed to us, and in contradiction to the posters adorning the walls of the hospital, Ann and Davey were denied the opportunity to practice feeding on demand while they remained in hospital. Instead, Davey was placed, without any consultation, on a four-hourly feeding regime. This set up quite a bizarre situation where, sometimes, Davey would be asleep but would need to be woken because it was time for his four-hourly feed. At other times, Davey would be awake and alert and would be opening and shutting his mouth in what seemed to be a newborn baby's way of saying "What's for lunch?" but, because four hours hadn't elapsed since the last meal time, Ann wasn't able to feed Davey.

I distinctly remember arriving at the hospital one morning on, perhaps, the second day after Davey's birth. Ann was standing up beside the bed attending to Davey who was lying on the bed. Our first conversation for the day proceeded as though it was a scene from a surreal comedy:

John: Hi there. What are you doing?
Ann: Howdy. I'm changing Davey's nappy.
John: Why are you changing his nappy?
Ann: To wake him up.
John: Why do you want to wake him up?
Ann: Because it's time for his feed.
John: Oh, OK (said with a puzzled tone).

During Ann's and Davey's time in hospital we were presented with an ever changing parade of midwives and medical doctors (MDs). Mostly these health professionals were kind, interested, and attentive. Occasionally, Davey was poked, prodded, and stretched and his responses to all this attention indicated that he was healthy and at the appropriate benchmarks for his time.

After a few days, however, we were informed, following a routine weighing, that Davey had lost 13% of his birth weight. The MD who told us this said that weight loss of that magnitude didn't bother him at all. He explained that the standards being used were norms that were established with post World War II bottle fed babies so he was relaxed about Davey's feeding and development. After that conversation, however, we didn't see that MD again.

The next MD we saw had quite a different attitude. He was concerned about Davey's weight loss and advised us that we should start supplementing the breast milk Davey was having with formula from a bottle. Ultimately we were not opposed to Davey being fed formula if he needed to be but both Ann and I felt that we hadn't persisted with breastfeeding for a sufficient period of time to judge whether or not we needed to add something extra. This MD, however, conveyed a sense of urgency in the situation. He ordered blood tests of Davey's blood to be taken and communicated to us that Davey's sodium and potassium levels were outside the expected ranges and "dangerously" so. He warned us that Davey could start fitting if these levels were not corrected swiftly.

In the midst of this hype, we were also in regular conversations with the midwives who, generally, were calm and helpful. They assured us that, once we were able to return to the familiarity and comfort of our own home, many of the feeding problems we were experiencing would disappear. After a week in hospital I suggested to the MD that we should have a night at home as a family. Our home was only a 20-minute drive from the hospital and I gave assurances that we would be back bright and early the next morning. The MD, however, cautioned that it would be "irresponsible" of him to "allow" us to leave the hospital. I asked if he was detaining us. He emphasised that he was not but reiterated that we would not be able to leave the hospital until Davey's "levels" were restored.

Instead of going home, Davey was transferred across the passageway to the Intensive Care Unit (ICU) where his four-hourly feeding regime was changed to a three-hourly protocol. We could visit Davey there as often as we wanted but were not able to stay with him in the unit so the medical staff took a polaroid photo of him and handed that to us. As the nurse slowly wheeled Davey in a crib from the ward room down the corridor and across the passageway to the ICU with Ann and I walking along behind, we both had the feeling that this seemed like a funeral march. We had the very strong sense that there was something seriously wrong with Davey that we were not being told and that he was probably going to die in the ICU.

When we arrived at the ICU the MD said that he wanted to put Davey on a drip to restore his sodium and potassium levels quickly. I asked how much more quickly the levels would be corrected on a drip as opposed to just being fed more regularly. The MD told me that this information was unknown. I then explained that I wouldn't give permission for Davey to be put on a drip if the MD wasn't able to provide evidence that being on a drip would alter Davey's levels much more quickly than simply feeding him more frequently. It seemed to me that a drip was an invasive and unnecessary procedure. The MD instructed that I would need to discuss this with the Consultant who was currently at another hospital and wouldn't be back until later in the afternoon. I said I was prepared to wait. Curiously, the drip was never mentioned again.

The same silliness that occurred on the four-hourly feeding cycle was repeated on the three-hourly cycle. I remember cradling Davey and singing to him at 9.55pm on the night that he was in the ICU because he was awake and making those mouth opening and shutting gestures. I asked if he could be fed but, the three hour limit hadn't been reached yet so I was told to wait. At about 10.05pm Davey seemed to have drifted off to sleep and at 10.15pm one of the nurses appeared to announce that it was time for Davey to be fed.

Davey had blood tests during the night and again in the morning. The MD who was working the night shift was an engaging and supportive woman with a strong German accent. This new MD gave us the *opposite* information from what the previous MD had provided us with regarding which one it was of Davey's sodium and potassium levels we should be most concerned about. Thankfully, on the ward round the next morning we were advised by a new Consultant that Davey's sodium and potassium levels were satisfactory and Ann and Davey would be discharged the next day.

Once we arrived home, after Ann and Davey were settled I visited the chemist and bought all the necessary supplies that we thought we would need to augment the nutrition Davey was receiving from breastfeeding. We never needed to use them. The midwives had been exactly right. From the time we were back at home, Ann and Davey established their own routine and Davey breastfed contentedly for the next three years, gradually weening himself when the time was right for him.

Although there were aspects to the care provided in hospital that were appropriate and satisfactory, the overzealous interventionist attitude of the MD with whom we had the most contact made the experience harrowing and distressing. As we were preparing to leave the hospital, one of the midwives asked our permission to record the details of our experience in a report. She too felt that our care had been less than ideal and she wanted it officially documented. Ann and Davey experienced inappropriate care through the overtreatment they received.

The ten day hospital experience could have been greatly improved by focussing on the perspectives of Ann and Davey. Even as a brand new baby, Davey's perspective should have been considered and honoured. Davey probably didn't have a perspective about a great many things back then but he certainly seemed to have an opinion about when he needed to be fed. This opinion was routinely dismissed in hospital yet, in the comfort of our own home, it was expected, sought, and encouraged.

The message from our experience is simple and one that has been explained throughout the book. Health professionals need to seek to learn about the perspectives of the people with whom they are working. If care is to be experienced as caring by the people to whom it is being administered then it has to be consistent with their priorities, preferences, and values. Even tiny little babies have ideas about the way they want things to be. Corrective efforts should definitely be introduced if required but, in order to understand whether they are required or not, the perspective of the individual is key. There is no other way to understand what correcting is needed. To adapt a slogan from Jiminy Cricket, in order to work effectively as a health professional, it's not your conscience, but the patient's perspective, that should always be your guide.

Jasmine's story

As a survivor of Bipolar and Obsessive Compulsive Disorder I feel that my illness fuels my practice as an artist. My artwork is frequently centred around making sense of traumatic life experiences and exploring the emotional hurdles I encounter on my non-linear journey of recovery. I believe passionately that the arts hold great holistic potential, predominantly through their ability to validate, explore, and disseminate personal narratives. I feel that the only way the stigma surrounding mental health will ever be broken down is through spreading awareness and having an open and ongoing dialogue surrounding what it really means to suffer mental distress.

It is also important for me to acknowledge that to many people, unusual experiences can be a gift, allowing us to experience extreme ends of the spectrum of human emotion and live with an outlook on life that many people will never possess. With great pain and distress, there also comes wisdom, a wealth of life experiences, and a unique opportunity for self-discovery. Through battling my disorder I have gained insight into the strength and resilience I possess to fight to stay alive and engaged with the world around me.

My ability to self-care has been nurtured by years of support from services, yet for many this vital support never materialises. It is far too difficult to obtain a referral for talking therapies and support for mental health problems. It takes an assertive attitude and boundless conviction to be taken seriously by most GPs and for many people this is an impossibly draining task. Being told to wait it out and see if things improve is a dismissal of the help-seeker's struggle and leaves many people feeling that they are alone in their suffering, with no viable way out.

Seeking help is a daunting process and if you are fortunate enough to be referred and begin therapy there is very little flexibility regarding appointment schedules, duration of treatment, and timeframe. The entire process leaves many people feeling stripped of autonomy and creates a situation whereby help is only available on the basis of a strict set of conditions. Failing to comply with these conditions can result in discharge and you are left alone once again.

I was recently pressured into being discharged from a mental health care team, as I did not use my care-coordinator. This was solely because my therapist provided the care that a care-coordinator usually delivers, alongside the therapeutic work we did together. Service providers, however, decided that not using my care-coordinator meant I no longer needed one, so I was discharged and left with no immediate access to support and no up to date care plan in place. This is a direct example of the rigidity of mental health services in defining how help must be used.

The consequences of this decision have been that I have become extremely unwell and have been visited by crisis and urgent care teams several times in a four-month period. A huge burden has fallen solely on my partner which has contributed directly to his health deteriorating and worsening his personal struggles with depression and anxiety. Furthermore, I have encountered financial hardship and struggled to undertake practical tasks such as filing tax returns and submitting benefit related paperwork. Tasks such as these are usually completed with the support of a care-coordinator.

As I wait to be assigned a new care team, I have reflected upon past experiences of support from mental health services and have found that, on many occasions, the care I received fell short of best practice.

When complaining of side effects from medication I have experienced a rebuttal technique that would make most politicians proud. I was made to feel that enormous weight gain (due to Olanzapine) was irrelevant to my well-being, and my sound mind and stability were deemed more important. This approach is incredibly damaging for numerous reasons. Primarily it demonstrates a lack of viewing my mental health as being intrinsically linked to my physical health. Secondly, the dismissal of my poor self-esteem and self-loathing as a result of drastic weight gain shows a complete lack of acknowledging that good physical health can lead to improvement in mood and self-worth. Refusal to see this means that my recovery was compartmentalised, with the priority of deciding what matters to me to achieve positive well-being, taken out of my hands.

There is often very little transparency in treatment and this is something that could be easily combatted by making more information readily available. Resources detailing how therapies work and what their delivery entails would be helpful. This information should make it clear that, for many people, the first few weeks of talking therapy can be very draining and distressing before it reaches the point of making a positive difference.

Predominantly, the greatest improvement to care provisions will arise from recognising and validating the experiences of service users in relation to their care so that their voices are *actually* being heard. Failure to genuinely pay attention to the service user's experiences feeds into a dichotomy between the patient as weak and helpless without the means to be an active agent in their recovery, and the clinician, a benevolent caregiver who holds all the knowledge and power to deliver relief from mental distress if they are obeyed. This unhelpful relationship can be demonstrated through the way in which many mental health practitioners see a patient's reluctance to stay on medication (which has been deemed to be unhelpful by the patient) as "active disengagement" from care, and symptomatic of a reluctance to achieve wellness. In fact, what is actually taking place in this instance is an example of the patient being autonomous over their own care, and actively expressing their knowledge that the medication is not right for them. The patient's perspective will only be considered when the patient's insights on this matter are recognised for what they are; "active engagement" with services and support. Obtaining information from patients about how the medication is being experienced by them is extremely useful for appropriate and effective treatment and should be sought at every opportunity, not minimised or dismissed.

Furthermore, mental health practitioners must be more aware of existing avenues of support based within the patient's own community. My carer has been without support for five years now, and every practitioner we have encountered has been ill equipped with the knowledge about who can meet his needs. Details of: support groups; subsidised complementary healthcare (massage, acupuncture, etc.); free exercise classes; subsidised relationship counselling; specific finance related education and support; patient involvement in mental health trusts; and so on should all be collected into a regularly updated resource, available freely for practitioners to distribute when required.

It is critical that patients are seen as people with the ability to have agency within their care. The main goal of mental health practitioners must be working to serve patients, this can only be achieved through recognising the wealth of knowledge and experience possessed by patients and using this to influence and inform the practice of mental health services. People who experience mental health problems are still people who know what they want and don't want. Mental health professionals could do a lot more to listen and learn from the people they are providing services to and to modify the services they are offering based on the information their patients provide.

Alex's story

Alex has always been different from other kids. Perhaps the other kids are "normal". And I was brought up to respect authority figures. I realise now these two things may not be a great combination. When the staff at Alex's daycare centre first "red flagged" Alex, I was a good girl and did what I was supposed to do. (The red flags were for his speech and the fact that he didn't play with other kids at daycare.)

As instructed, I went to my GP to get a referral for Alex to a paediatrician. With the necessary referral we went off to the paediatrician for an assessment. The paediatrician seemed nice enough at first. Alex played happily while she asked me lots of questions. During the conversation, Alex occasionally came over to give me a hug and tell me he loved me. The paediatrician considered the red flag and advised that the first thing to do was to get Alex's hearing tested. If Alex's hearing was all OK, then the paediatrician thought Alex would benefit from a speech and language assessment and probably some therapy. That was the extent of her initial advice. I was quite happy to go along with these suggestions; Alex's speech was definitely hard to understand and, at times, he would get quite frustrated by this. To be honest, after this first appointment I was impressed and relieved that she didn't try to tell me that Alex was autistic.

Shortly after this, during the transition program for entry into the first year of school (Prep), I heard a behavioural optometrist give a talk on how an assessment can help identify issues before a child starts school. So, being the mother I am (who wants to do the best for her kids), I dutifully booked Alex in for an assessment. I figured that any insight into Alex and how to help him in school would be a good thing. I explained as I was booking the assessment that Alex has a language delay. The optometrist assured me that would not be a problem – not an issue, we can work around that.

So we turned up for the assessment. The first part was fine – standard eye chart stuff. Alex can already read (way ahead of his peers) so we had that covered. The second part, however, was more physical. The optometrist asked Alex to do things like keep his head still and just follow with his eyes (instead, Alex waved his head around like one of those Sideshow Alley clowns) and push down against the optometrist's arms (that's not happening either). Then, the optometrist asked Alex to stand in the middle of the room. Well, Alex looked vaguely at him and had no idea what he was talking about. As his best guess, Alex copied the optometrist then, when that didn't work, he moved to where the optometrist was pointing. Alex had no idea of what this man was asking. The worst part was that the optometrist seemed completely oblivious to the fact that Alex didn't understand him. I thought to myself "*This is the part where he has a language delay you dingleberry*". At that point, the optometrist lost my respect. When the assessment had been completed, the optometrist told me that Alex had preprio something (I couldn't remember what the other syllables were) and low tone and I should get him checked for Praeder-Willi Syndrome. By this stage, whether he was good at his job or not or had anything of value to offer me in terms of Alex's development, he had lost me. I was no longer taking it in. I paid the scheduled $160 and was inwardly fuming at the waste of money and time. I politely declined the offer for a written report for another $30 and I paid little attention to their comment that they would email me a reminder for another check in a year's time. Instead, I was thinking *"Reminder to self: block their email address"*.

When I arrived home I consulted Dr Google to find out what Praeder–Willi Syndrome is. I burst into tears and blocked the optometrist's email address.

After my experience with the behavioural optometrist I was a lot more cautious about placing my trust in health professionals. I did some research before selecting a place to test Alex's hearing. I wanted to find a place that actually dealt with kids and knew what they were doing. I located a service that worked with children who were deaf from birth. Awesome experience. The staff made sure Alex was comfortable by taking five minutes or so to chat with him and let him choose a game. Furthermore, they made sure he understood what they wanted him to do and if he didn't, they showed him. Amazing! Alex went into a booth and performed like a champion. His hearing is perfect.

Next was the speech assessment. The GP had recommended a good one. So off we went. The woman conducting the assessment was good with Alex, but had to earn her money. After the first ten minutes, Alex didn't want to play anymore. There were good toys that were much more interesting than the assessment tasks but Alex completed the assessment by being enticed with reward games. I was shocked when I got the report saying that Alex had a severe language delay. I didn't think he was that bad. The report recommended either getting Alex on a waiting list with the Health Department or finding a private speech therapist close to home so he could have regular therapy.

By this stage it was time to go back to the paediatrician for a follow-up appointment. At the appointment I mentioned that I'd taken Alex to the behavioural optometrist after the school talk and that he had said Alex had low tone and preprio something. The paediatrician said "God I wish they wouldn't tell parents to go to those people". I was a little taken aback. I asked if a physiotherapist might help Alex with his muscle tone. The paediatrician replied with a comment that it wouldn't hurt if we wanted to spend the money but she wasn't enthusiastic about it. She did recommend a local speech therapist and we agreed to another review appointment when she returned from maternity leave.

Despite the paediatrician's lack of encouragement, I found a paediatric physiotherapist after a few months (they're as scarce as hen's teeth) and took Alex for an assessment. The physiotherapist got him to do some exercises and run up and down a few times. She said Alex was hyperflexible and got me to listen to him run so I could hear the flip, flop as he ran. She also showed me how Alex can touch his thumb to his arm. The physiotherapist confirmed that he had that preprio whatsit thing and that he was much stronger on one side of his body and favoured that side.

After this assessment we organised fortnightly sessions, where the physiotherapist worked with Alex and gave us exercises to do at home. He made good progress but is still clumsy and can't ride a bike yet. Despite this, the sessions felt productive – the physiotherapist explained the what and the why of what she was doing and gave me options so I could do something about it. In addition to these sessions, we took Alex to Flip Out (indoor trampolines) on a weekly basis and he made great gains with evening up his strong and weak sides. The physiotherapist was really encouraging about this and explained that you can't be uncoordinated on a trampoline and it would be really helping him. She urged us to keep it up. Unfortunately, due to the physiotherapist's availability, we weren't able to continue the sessions we were having but this was one of the best interactions I've had with health professionals. Ironically, if I had paid attention to the paediatrician, I would never have made an appointment.

At about this time, Alex's teachers at school started "making noises" about Alex. They requested meetings and had various ideas and opinions about Alex. From then on it felt like

I had both the health system and the education system to contend with. In both systems I've found that there's no shortage of advice but it's rare for me to be asked what I want or what I think might be going on or should happen.

By this stage, our next appointment with the paediatrician had come around again. The paediatrician acknowledged that Alex had made some progress but, from her perspective, it was not enough. She recommended an assessment to test for autism. I'd been dreading the "A" word and my hackles went up. I don't think Alex is autistic. He doesn't display repetitive behaviours. The only place he has issues is in the classroom. I asked what an assessment like this would actually achieve. Apparently I would get money (the paediatrician explained that, with an assessment, Alex could get autism funding until he was seven) and he would get a teacher's aide at school. I wouldn't have to pay for the speech therapist and physiotherapist anymore – it would come out of his funding. OK. The money is fine, but I was interested in knowing what would actually change for Alex. The paediatrician's response was to reiterate "Well you'd get money". So Alex would get no effective change. Thoughts started swirling around in my mind. There will be nothing different to help him with his development. Are there no suggestions for other therapies to try? What about brain mapping to see where his strengths and weaknesses are? What about therapies that harness neuroplasticity to improve speech? Nothing. It's just about the money. The sum extent of all our smart monkey brains and medical research is to slap a label on him and throw some money at it.

I politely told the paediatrician that I would think about it. I left the appointment with my mind already made up that I wouldn't be going back.

Months later, Alex got sick and we visited our GP. While we were there, the GP suggested going back to the paediatrician for a review. The GP didn't seem interested in what our experience of the paediatrician had been but just assumed we needed to return. I explained that it was difficult with busy schedules but the GP encouraged me to go back because the paediatrician was concerned about Alex's speech. I didn't make an appointment to see the paediatrician and I haven't been back to the GP since.

My rollercoaster ride with the health and education systems continues. In the wee hours of the morning (every goddamn morning) I lie awake worrying about Alex and wonder if what I'm doing is the best thing for him. I was so anti-diagnosis because I think it's bullshit and, for Alex, it's all about making him conform to the world. But the thought of him being mistreated and getting picked on at school upsets me a lot. I can't control what happens at school and I feel like I am exposing him to danger, fear, or victimisation when it's my job to protect him. Maybe we should just get the stupid diagnosis so I know he's ok; he can build a relationship with a teacher's aide (which is how you get the best out of him), he might even like going to school then. Everyone assumes he's autistic anyway, or retarded because he's so big for his age. Then when he gets upset at loud noises or when he makes a mistake, someone will be there to comfort him when I can't be there. If he has a diagnostic label I won't have to sit in the waiting room at the new GP surgery, trembling with the anticipation that they're going to say something about him maybe being "on the spectrum" – which has already occurred.

Whatever happens next I won't be going back to the paediatrician. Alex's brother Martin has had some sessions with an awesome psychologist. She listens to me and Martin, she asks what we want to achieve, what we are working through, and what we need her help with. She and Martin work together and he has made great progress. In fact, I'm thinking of getting an appointment for myself and talking to her about Alex. I really don't like discussing my feelings and fears and problems though so it might be a while before I summon the courage to make the appointment.

My experiences haven't been all bad but they've definitely been characterised by health professionals and educators generally making judgments and decisions without involving me or Alex or checking with us about what we want. I don't know why it's so difficult to ask me what I want or what I think but, in my experience, it's rare for that to happen. More than anything, I would like the health professionals to listen to me and to help Alex build on the many strengths that he has. We'll get there. I'm convinced of that. It would just be nice if the health professionals felt more like allies than adversaries. I know they mean well but when they don't pay attention to what we want it just feels like a battle.

Donna's story

In 1988 I became pregnant with my only daughter. She was born in Katherine in 1989 by Caesarean section. I was 21 years old and this was the only operation I had ever had in my life at that time.

When I found a new partner three years later, I wanted to have another baby. It still wasn't happening, so I arranged to have a thorough check up to find out what was causing the problem. The gynaecologist said that he would put dye in my tubes to see if they were blocked. I went to have the procedure and I could see what they were doing as I wasn't heavily sedated. The doctor told me that it would hurt if my tubes were blocked. As the procedure started I felt horrific pain and the doctor looked at the screen and said "Oh you silly thing, you've had your tubes tied". I could see the tie on both sides. I was horrified and shocked. I couldn't believe what I was hearing. I said "Hey doctor! I have never consented to having my tubes tied. I've only had one operation and that was when I had my daughter". He said that he could see that my tubes were tied. I explained to the doctor that I had never given permission to have my tubes tied. I was only 21 years old, don't they only do something like that when there is sufficient cause? I said I'm too young to have that done. The doctor investigated a little further. The medical staff who did my caesarean said that tying my tubes wasn't on their job list and they didn't do it. I was booked in for another procedure to have my tubes untied. When I came out, I was told they couldn't do it. Then they said that I must have had pelvic inflammatory disease and because it was untreated, it messed up my tubes. I said that couldn't be the case as when I first became pregnant all the necessary tests for sexually transmitted diseases were completed.

This was a very testing time in my life. I just couldn't believe what I was hearing. I had about another three operations. Even the micro surgeon said it appeared that my tubes had been cut. No one, however, would clearly say or put in writing that this had actually been done. I got upset and "went off". I said "Is this what you people do to Aboriginal women, so we can't breed kids?" I let them know that they made me feel like a dirty, unruly woman who had a sexual disease that was never treated.

I was advised to go out of the Northern Territory (NT) to seek legal advice and to sue the health professionals who were responsible but I was sick of being operated on. I had so much scarring both physically and emotionally that no matter what amount of money or exposure I would get about this, it wouldn't change the fact that my daughter wouldn't be blessed with another sibling from me. It took a long time but I got over it. I never held any grudges but now I do not trust any medical people and always get a second opinion.

I felt that the care I experienced in terms of the operation in which my tubes were tied was not legal because there was no consent provided. For my personal story, I didn't want to go on contraception, I wanted to have a few more kids that were close in age, but I was not able to do this. No matter what happened, I couldn't get pregnant.

This less than ideal care impacted on my ability to have children and to create the family that I wanted. To compound the problem, hearing from the health staff that I may have had an infection and that this was part of the reason why the operation could not have been reversed was devastating. And the way these health professionals had this conversation with me was traumatic in nature.

It shouldn't be asking too much to expect health professionals to work in legal, ethical, culturally safe, and moral ways in their health work but this would greatly improve their health practices. Health professionals need to talk to their patients with more care, compassion, and foresight. Importantly, talking without judging would improve the psychological care towards patients, even when the news is not so good.

Health professionals need to understand that care and compassion go a long way. They need to know more about the people they work with. They need to refrain from judging others and work in a non-assuming way. It would be wonderful if they did not hold stigmatising attitudes towards Aboriginal and Torres Strait Islander peoples. Medical staff need to treat people as they would their own family. If that was the case, the health professionals would make sure they completely understood what had happened, why it had happened, and they would delve further if needed.

Health professionals need to understand that Aboriginal and Torres Strait Islander people are people just like them. They have hopes and desires and dreams and goals. Their hopes and dreams might be different to yours but they are no less important to them as yours are to you. Aboriginal and Torres Strait Islander people have the same rights as other Australians to access the resources and support they need to build their dreams and achieve their goals.

Concluding comments

Five very different stories but five remarkably similar messages. It's clear from these accounts that health care is not routinely poor, but it is just as apparent that it could always be improved. It is no coincidence that, in these stories, where there were examples of care that was not poor, it had the characteristics of patient-perspective care.

In each of these reports, routinely and persistently focussing on the perspective of the person receiving the service and providing support and advice to help them achieve their goals would have led to very different experiences for the people involved. These are five powerful illustrations of why it is so imperative to replace our patient-centred health care systems with patient-perspective systems. It is critical that, instead of emphasising where the patient is situated geographically, we focus on the patient's perspective. The provision of appropriate health care demands that we have an appreciation of the patient's values, priorities, and preferences. The sustainability of our services and the health of the populations of our planet depend on it.

9

WHERE TO FROM HERE?

Inappropriate care is the global scourge of health systems. Our current health services can be characterised by both the overtreatment *and* the undertreatment of populations. Sometimes, bizarrely, overtreatment and undertreatment occur concurrently within the same service. As a result of this inappropriate care, people are harmed rather than helped, and billions of dollars are wasted annually.

Throughout this book, I have outlined the nature of the inappropriate care problem, and I've described a solution. Patient-centred care has not provided a pathway to the routine provision of appropriate care. Care that is formulated and provided appropriately must be shaped by the preferences, values, and priorities of the people to whom it is being administered. The patient-centred framework emphasises where the patient is situated geographically, but having the patient at the centre of health professionals' deliberations does not guarantee that the patient's point of view will define the decision making that occurs. It is the perspective of the patient, not her position, that is paramount. Thus, patient-perspective care rather than patient-centred care is the paradigm that is necessary to haul us out of the quagmire in which we currently languish.

To be sure, some health professionals quite naturally attend to the opinions of patients. Furthermore, some isolated programs and services occasionally appear which seem to be driven by patient's wishes. By and large, however, these trends are not occurring on the scale that is required to redirect the course of the behemoth of global health care. These initiatives are encouraging because they demonstrate what can be achieved, but they merely tease, in a tantalisingly optimistic way, of what a brighter future for health systems and services could be. We can now generalise a specific point made at the close of the last chapter with regard to the five stories described in that chapter. When health care is effective and appropriate, it is probably already embodying patient-perspective principles. We need to learn from examples of patient-perspective best practice and apply our learning to all health services and systems.

The blueprint that outlines the means by which the current model of health service delivery can be overturned in favour of a model that is consistent with our design as controlling agents must be exhaustive. It must include the training programs of health professionals as well as the policies that govern health professionals' practices. Additionally, there must be ongoing, accurate, and accessible education programs for those who access health services. These programs should start in schools but should also be available to the general public.

Education and training of health professionals

A health system overhaul of the magnitude that is required will clearly affect the training of health professionals at university as well as their ongoing professional development after they have completed their initial training. Of course, standard information about the nature of illness and disease and the treatment options for which there is the best evidence will be essential. Just as crucial, however, will be substantial training in communication with an emphasis on considered curiosity for the purpose of learning. Health professionals will need extensive experience at considering the words a patient is offering them in the context of other information they will learn to pay attention to. A constant theme throughout all training experiences will be the autonomy and capability of the patients the health professionals serve.

Training in assessment and history taking, for example, will prioritise learning about the patient rather than learning about the disease or illness. This attitude is very much in the spirit of William Osler's sage advice. Frequently described as the "father of modern medicine", Osler famously said, "It is much more important to know what sort of a patient has a disease than what sort of a disease a patient has" (www.brainyquote.com/quotes/quotes/w/williamosl391388.html). Armed with the theoretical background of Perceptual Control Theory, health professionals will be adept at developing an awareness of patients in the contexts within which patients are situated in terms of the lives they are forging for themselves and the impact their current ailments have on their living as they would wish it to be.

Understanding goals and how they function will also be a necessary part of a patient-perspective health professional's learning. Health professionals such as these will become expert goal setters themselves but will also appreciate the role they can play in helping others achieve important goals. Learning about the process of goal attainment and the functioning of an interconnected hierarchy of goals will necessarily involve recognising how goal realisation can be hampered through both internal and external factors. Health professionals being trained within a patient-perspective paradigm will grasp the limitations of concepts such as empathy and goal sharing and will discern with care, compassion, and precision the bounds of their skills and expertise and the reach of their influence.

The importance of the initial training of health professionals should not be underestimated. The ultimate challenge will be to provide neophyte health professionals with the information and other resources they need to overturn beliefs and attitudes about the wisdom and authority of people in their positions. The development of attitudes of reflection and scepticism will be emphasised over the skills of advice giving and compliance promotion. Budding health professionals will be taught to encourage and endorse questioning from their patients and will become acquainted with the discomfort of being disagreed with. Fundamentally, the future leaders of our health services and systems will learn to value a service that serves rather than one that steers.

Policy changes

Changes to local and global policies will support the new direction in training. Health service managers will need to reconfigure priorities, and policymakers will be required to ensure that policies consistently reflect and endorse a patient-perspective model. At a general level, policies will accurately reflect where responsibilities lie. As was illustrated in Chapter 6 with the Council of Australian Governments' *Closing the Gap* policy, it is *not* the responsibility of governments to improve the health of the people being governed. Rather, it is the responsibility of individuals, families, and communities to improve their own health, and it is the responsibility of governments to ensure the necessary resources are available so the citizens of these governments can live the lives of their own design. Patient-perspective policies will specify that it is the government's duty to *routinely monitor and evaluate* resource provision and to improve resource provision as required and where necessary. Health outcomes may still be of some interest but only to indicate where resource allocation could be bolstered.

Problems with specific policies such as the National Institute for Health and Clinical Excellence (NICE) guidelines (NICE, 2009) were discussed in Chapter 3. Guidelines such as these would be reviewed and revised to embody the patient-perspective ethos. Currently, the guidelines endorse a patient-centred approach and the problems with this endorsement are evident in statements such as: "Treatment and care should take into account patients' needs and preferences" (NICE, 2009, p. 8). It might even be difficult for health professionals steeped in the patient-centred tradition to detect the problem with this simple statement. In a patient-perspective world, patients' needs and preferences wouldn't merely be "taken into account" as though you were accommodating someone's predilection for having his eye-fillet cooked medium rare. The patient-perspective paradigm demands that patients' perspectives *define* the health care that is provided.

Other statements throughout the guidelines similarly reveal how deficient they are in terms of providing treatments that can be used by patients to achieve important goals. For example, on page 22 (NICE, 2009), section 1.5.1.3 states that:

The choice of intervention should be influenced by the:

- duration of the episode of depression and the trajectory of symptoms
- previous course of depression and response to treatment
- likelihood of adherence to treatment and any potential adverse effects
- person's treatment preference and priorities

While it is encouraging that preferences and priorities are mentioned at all, the emphasis is, again, misguided. Treatment preferences and priorities are the fourth out of four bullet points when aspects of the depression have been considered along with the likelihood of adherence to treatment. If treatment preferences and priorities are determining treatment decisions, however, it makes no sense to discuss adherence probabilities. Again, the patient's perspectives are not being held in the esteem which is required for the provision of appropriate care. Then, on page 26 (NICE, 2009), the guidelines declare that "the aim of treatment is to obtain significant improvement or remission" (p. 26). The aim of any treatment in a patient-perspective habitat, however, would be to enable the recipient of the treatment to live the life he chooses.

Practice guidelines and policy statements, therefore, would need to be dramatically overhauled to advance the imperative of patient-perspective care. It is not enough to simply mention words such as "preference" and "priority". Every word and every sentence in every policy directive needs to consistently uphold the authority of the patient's perspective.

Public education initiatives

As has been mentioned throughout this book, changing the way in which we communicate with patients will be a non-negotiable feature of adopting the patient-perspective system. An important component in reshaping health care will be the education of the people who access health services. The general population will need to be educated and informed differently from the way they are now. Sustained and comprehensive campaigns will advise people of their rights to be the drivers of their health care. Accessible and easily understood brochures and flyers will be plentiful and will cover the range of health problems and health services available. The possible harms of overtreatment as well as the limitations of screening tests will be widely discussed. Discerning and sceptical attitudes will be encouraged, and seeking further opinions will be welcomed.

An excellent example of the resources that will be common-place in a patient–perspective health care system is the website www.rxisk.org. The purpose of this website is to make medicine safer for everyone by providing information and a forum for people to discuss their experiences with medication. On the home page of the website are the statements: "No one knows a prescription drug's side effects like the person taking it"; "Make your voice heard"; and "RxISK is a free, independent drug safety website to help you weigh the benefits of any medication against its potential dangers". People can access this website to obtain information about the medications they are taking so they are well placed to make appropriate decisions about the balance of benefits and harms and the acceptability of the medication from their point of view.

It will undoubtedly take time as well as clever and multi-pronged approaches for people to realise that their views are critical to the effectiveness and efficiency of the health care they receive. Perhaps it will even be the case that some people will be suspicious at first of this invitation to be the director, producer, and choreographer of their own health care show. A sustained, steadfast, and sincere attitude on the part of the health professionals will be necessary for people who are patients to notice the invitation. They may, in fact, only notice that something different is afoot through the inertia that will exist regarding service provision without *their* hands at the steering wheel and *their* foot on the accelerator pedal.

My final word – for now!

Despite how extensive this service redesign will need to be, it should not be thought of as a revolution. Typically, in a revolution, there is an initial new idea; then some upheaval and disruption; and then, over time, conditions *revolve back to* something very similar to the situation that existed before the revolution.

Adopting a patient-perspective model of health service delivery will take us to a very different place from where we are now. This will be a place where effective and efficient health care is universally available and routinely expected.

Ironically, even though health systems will be radically and thoroughly reformed by a patient-perspective approach, the greatest change that may be required is an attitudinal reorganisation on the part of health professionals. Recognising the importance of following the lead of the patient, and providing support as required, rather than being the captain and decision maker of the treatment that is delivered, may be the most profound change of all. Without this change, all other efforts at correcting the problem will be futile. When this change occurs, however, many other aspects of service reconfiguration will fall into place as the domino effect creates a health service that is genuinely a service from the perspective of the people who are accessing it. When this occurs, the flagrant waste of billions of dollars annually through the provision of inappropriate care as well as the consequent harms to patients will be arrested. Only then will people be able to reasonably expect health services that promote rather than prevent the living they crave.

Reference

NICE. (2009). *Depression: The treatment and management of depression in adults.* London, UK: National Institute for Health and Clinical Excellence. Retrieved June 27, 2017, from nice.org.uk/guidance/cg90

Index

Page numbers in bold indicate a table on the corresponding page.

Aboriginal persons 36–40, 72, 78
Allison, P. J. 36
American Psychiatric Association
    (APA) 24
American Psychological
    Association **66**
appointments *see* patient-led
    appointment scheduling
appropriate care, definition of 5–6;
    see also patient-perspective care
Ardilo, A. 40
Australian Psychological Society **66**

Barkham, M. 27
Beck, Aaron T. 88
bibliotherapy 27
Binnie, J. 28
biomedical model 11–12
Borglin, G. 41
Bower, P. 27

Breslin 27–28
British Psychological Society **66**
Brownlee, S. 2, 11, 13, 23; on balance
    between benefits and harms
    41–42; on definitions of disease
    and abnormality leading to
    overdiagnosis 75; on the grey zone
    4–6; on patient goals 14

Canadian Psychological
    Association **67**
Carey, T. A. 53
Casey, L. M. 83
Cassels, A. 76
Chassin, M. R. 2, 3
Claire, A. 77
Closing the Gap 78, 125
Clough, B. A. 83
communication, listening and
    believing in 34–35

control: of destiny 65; examples in nature 51–52; health and 52–53; important features of phenomenon of 50–51; mechanisms of 47–50
Council of Australian Governments (COAG) 78, 125
Crazy Like Us: The Globalization of the Western Mind 36
cultural, social, and emotional well-being (CSEWB) 38
cultural considerations in patient's perspective 36–40

Department of Veterans Affairs, US 18
Devaraj, V. S. 83
Dewing, J. 18
diagnosis: contributing to problem of inappropriate care 24–25; over- 23
Diagnostic and Statistical Manual of Mental Disorders (DSM-5) 24
dynamic nature of life 35–36

education and training health professionals 69–70, 123–125
empathy 55, 60–61
empowerment, patient 74–75

Feine, J. S. 36
Feng, Q. 83
Fried, E. I. 24

Galvin, R. W. 2, 3
Garcia-Armesto, S. 11, 13, 25, 26, 75
Gbolade, B. A. 83
Gilbody, S. 27
Glover, G. 23
goals, patient 13
Golden Rule 55, 57–60
Gotzsche, P. 6, 11
grey zone in health care 3–6
Griffith, G. M. 68

Haley, J. 86
Hastings, R. P. 68
health and control 52–53
health care crisis, global 1, 122–123; defining appropriate care and 5–6; defining important terms in 2–3; factors leading to 10–16; failure of concept of patient-centred care and 17–28; grey zone 3–6; pervasiveness and cost of inappropriate care in 2; *see also* inappropriate care
health professionals, education and training of 69–70, 123–125
Hutchinson, L. 68

Improving Accessing to Psychological Therapies (IAPT) 23, 28, 40–41
inappropriate care 32–33, 122–123; acknowledging the impact of the power imbalance in 13–15; current situation of 15–16; diagnosis contributing to problem of 24–25; downside to biomedical model and 11–12; factors in development of 10–16; misuse of norms in 12–13; pervasiveness and cost of 2; quality of life and 33–34; *see also* health care crisis, global; patient-centred care
In Control blog 48
Institute of Medicine 17
intersubjectivity 62

Jachuck, S. J. 33, 68

Kheirkhah, P. 83
Kilfedder, C. 27

Lambert, M. 87
listening and believing in communication 34–35
Locker, D. 36

major depressive disorder (MDD)
24–25
Marks, Isaac 88
Marmot, M. 46
Marshall, D. 41, 84
McCance, T. 18
McCormack, B. 18
McQueen, D. 28
Method of Levels 88–91
Meuldijk, D. 22
missed appointments *see* patient-led
appointment scheduling
mistakes and risks management in
patient-perspective care 73–74
misuse: costs of 2; definition of 2–3;
grey zone 3–4; of norms 12–13
Moynihan, R. 76

*National Aboriginal and Torres Strait
Islander Health Plan* 72
*National Aboriginal Health Strategy,
A* 38
*National Framework for
Recovery-Oriented Mental Health
Services: Guide for Practitioners and
Providers, A* 63
*National Framework for Universal
Child and Family Health Services* 72
National Health Service (NHS) 40,
83, 84–85, 87, 91
National Institute for Health and
Clinical Excellence (NICE) 22,
23, 126
*National Practice Standards for the
Mental Health Workforce 2013* 64
Nesse, R. M. 24
norms, misuse of 12–13

objectivity 55, 61–62
Osler, William 124
overdiagnosis 23, 75–76
overmedicalisation 75–76
overuse 75–76; costs of 2; definition
of 2–3; grey zone 4

Palmer, J. 83
patient-centred care 6, 28, 122–123;
barriers to patient involvement in
25–26; clash between policy and
practice and 27–28; compared to
patient-perspective care 55–57;
definition of 17; disconnect
between treatment expectations
and actual delivery 19–20; failure
of concept of 17–28; language
of 18–19; patient-perspective
approach versus 7–8, 18; problems
with research methodology and
20–22; problems with use of
guidelines and 23; shared decision
making in 26–27
patient-led appointment scheduling:
Carey on getting interested in
84–85; continuing to search for
a rationale for 87–88; looking for
evidence on 85–87; problem with
missed appointments and 82–83;
program development 88–91;
results and conclusions 91–93;
system beginnings 87; trying to
remedy the situation of missed
appointments 83–84
patient-perspective care 7–8,
18, 32–33, 79–80, 128–129;
applying services or making
services available in 78–79;
balance between benefits and
harms and 41–42; compared
to patient-centred care 55–57;
cultural considerations in
36–40; decision-making about
treatment design and delivery in
70–71; education and training of
health professionals for 69–70,
123–125; empathy in 55, 60–61;
empowering patients in 74–75;
engaging or inviting patients to
participate in 71–73; Golden Rule
and 55, 57–60; importance of

values and preferences in 45–46; managing mistakes and risks in 73–74; missed appointments and 40–41, 82–83; objectivity in 55, 61–62; patient-led appointment scheduling in 82–93; patient stories on 96–121; policy changes for 125–127; in practice 55–80; public education initiatives 127–128; quality of life and 33–34; recognising the dynamic nature of things we have regarded as static in 35–36; self-determination in 63–67; standards in 75–77; theoretical underpinnings of 44–53; thinking about communication in terms of listening and believing in 34–35; and whose perspective from which to consider behavior in 68–69; *see also* Perceptual Control Theory (PCT)

patients: barriers to involvement in treatment decisions 25–26; health care goals of 13; power imbalance and 13–15; quality of life 33–34; shared decision making by 26–27; stories of perspectives of 96–121; "treatment dropout" 18–20, 40–41

patient stories 96–121; Alex's 112–118; Bronwyn's 100–103; Davey's 103–108; Donna's 118–120; Jasmine's 108–112

Perceptual Control Theory (PCT) 7, 46–50, 53, 124; functional models 47; how control works and 47–50; important features of phenomenon of control and 50–51; reasons for 46–47; self-determination and 64; standards and 77; and whose perspective from which to consider behavior in 68; *see also* patient-perspective care

Perry, S. 86–87

policy changes 125–127

power imbalance in health care 13–15; listening and believing and 34–35

Powers, W. T. 47, 51–52

psychological treatments 19–20, 22; diagnosis contributing to problem of inappropriate care in 24–25

Psychology Today 48

public education initiatives 127–128

quality of life, patient perspective on 33–34

randomised controlled trials (RCT) 20–22, 27

RCT (randomised controlled trials) 20–22

research, biomedical 11–12

Richards, D. A. 41

RxISK 128

Saini, V. 4–5, 11, 13–14, 25–26, 75

Saxby, P. 83

self-determination 63–67

Sharafkhaneh, A. 83

shared decision making 26–27

Smith, P. St. J. 28

SMS text messaging 83

Stone, C. 83

Syme, S. L. 65

Tavakoli-Tabasi, S. 83

text messaging 83

theoretical underpinnings of patient-perspective care 44–53; importance of values and preferences in 45–46

Torres Strait Islanders 36–40, 72, 78

Travis, L. M. 83

"treatment dropout" patients 18–20; missed appointments and 40–41

treatments: barriers to involvement of patients in decisions regarding 25–26; decisions in patient-perspective care 70–71; diagnosis contributing to problem of inappropriate care for 24–25; problems with guidelines 23; randomised controlled trials of 20–22, 27; shared decision making regarding 26–27; "treatment dropout" patients 18–20; *see also* patient-led appointment scheduling

underuse: costs of 2; definition of 2–3; grey zone 4

values and preferences in patient-perspective care 45–46
Velmans, M. 61–62

Watters, Ethan 36–37
Williams, C. H. 77
World Health Organization (WHO) 75

Your health. Your say. 73

For Product Safety Concerns and Information please contact our EU
representative GPSR@taylorandfrancis.com
Taylor & Francis Verlag GmbH, Kaufingerstraße 24, 80331 München, Germany

www.ingramcontent.com/pod-product-compliance
Lightning Source LLC
Chambersburg PA
CBHW050530270326
41926CB00015B/3158